Charles Coppens

A Brief Text-Book of Moral Philosophy

Charles Coppens

A Brief Text-Book of Moral Philosophy

ISBN/EAN: 9783337332785

Printed in Europe, USA, Canada, Australia, Japan

Cover: Foto ©Thomas Meinert / pixelio.de

More available books at **www.hansebooks.com**

A. M. D. G.

A BRIEF TEXT-BOOK

OF

MORAL PHILOSOPHY.

BY

REV. CHARLES COPPENS, S.J.,

Author of "A Brief Text-Book of Logic and Mental Philosophy," "A Practical Introduction to English Rhetoric," and "The Art of Oratorical Composition."

"The rule and measure of human acts is reason."--St. Thomas.

NEW YORK
SCHWARTZ, KIRWIN & FAUSS
42 Barclay Street

Copyright, 1895,

by

CATHOLIC SCHOOL BOOK COMPANY.

ALL RIGHTS RESERVED,

PREFACE.

This "Brief Text-Book of Moral Philosophy" is a companion volume to the author's "Brief Text-Book of Logic and Mental Philosophy," lately published and already extensively used in Academies and other educational institutions. The author's aim is to present to students and readers—to such, especially, as are unfamiliar with the Latin language—a brief yet clear outline of the system of Ethics taught in Catholic Colleges, Seminaries and Universities. This system is based on the philosophy of Aristotle.

Questions of Ethics, which in former times were left to the close scientific treatment of specialists, are at the present day freely discussed among all classes of society—in newspapers and popular magazines, in the workshop and in the parlor.

Extravagant notions of individual and social rights are circulated, while the rash speculations of so-called scientists are sapping in many minds the very foundations of morality. Never before has there been a more urgent call on the part of the people for the lucid exposition and the correct application of sound moral principles.

In this sad confusion of thought, no small utility will be found in a clear, simple, systematic explanation of the ethical doctrines taught by the greatest minds of the past ages, and lately most highly recommended by our Supreme Pontiff, the illustrious Leo. XIII. Such an exposition the author has endeavored to present in this little volume.

THE AUTHOR.

CREIGHTON UNIVERSITY, OMAHA, NEB.
March 12, 1895.

TABLE OF CONTENTS.

                                                PAGE

INTRODUCTION, ... 7

BOOK I—DIRECTION OF HUMAN ACTS.

CHAPTER I. **The End to which Human Acts are to be Directed:** 11
    Article I. Ends in General, ... 11
    " II. The Last End of Man, . . . 13
    " III. The Attainment of the Last End. . 20

CHAPTER II. **The Morality of Human Acts:** . . 27
    Article I. The Essence of Morality, . . . 27
    " II. The Determinants of Morality, . . 33
    " III. Accountability for Moral Acts, . . 36
    " IV. Circumstances that Lessen Accountability, ... 39
    " V. The Passions, ... 42
    " VI. Virtues and Vices. 45

CHAPTER III. **Law, the Rule of Human Acts:** . . 49
    Article I. The Moral Law, ... 49
    " II. Conscience, ... 57
    " III. Sanction of the Moral Law. . . 63

BOOK II.—INDIVIDUAL RIGHTS AND DUTIES.

CHAPTER I. **Rights and Duties in General.** . . 69
CHAPTER II. **Our Duties to God:** 74
    Article I. Adoration, ... 75
    " II. Faith in God, ... 77
    " III. Love of God. 84
CHAPTER III. **Our Duties to Ourselves.** . . . 86

	PAGE
CHAPTER IV. **Our Duties to Other Men:** . . .	89
Article I. Duty of Love to Others, . . .	89
" II. Duties Regarding the Minds and Wills of Others, ...	91
" III. Duties Regarding the Lives of Others,	95
" IV. Duties Regarding Honor. . . .	99
CHAPTER V. **Rights of Ownership:**	102
Article I. Validity of Titles to Ownership, .	102
" II. Violations of Ownership, . . .	109
" III. Various Modes of Acquiring Property,	110
" IV. Transfer of Property by Contract, .	112
" V. Wages of Laborers.	114

BOOK III.—SOCIAL RIGHTS AND DUTIES.

CHAPTER I. **Society in General.**	119
CHAPTER II. **Domestic Society:**	123
Article I. Nature and Purpose of Domestic Society, ...	123
" II. Unity and Indissolubility of Matrimony, ...	125
" III. Parental Authority—Education. .	130
CHAPTER III. **Civil Society:**	139
Article I. Nature and Origin of Civil Society: .	139
§ 1. The End of Civil Government,	139
§ 2. The Units that Compose Civil Society, ...	141
§ 3. Civil Authority, . . .	141
§ 4. Means Employed by Civil Authority.	145
Article II. The Functions of Civil Government:	146
§ 1. Legislation, ...	147
§ 2. The Judiciary, . . .	149
§ 3. The Executive. . . .	153
CHAPTER IV. **International Law.**	155

INTRODUCTION.

1. **Moral Philosophy** is the science of the moral order, or of the right and wrong of human acts. It is called *Ethics* from the Greek word ἤθη, which, like the Latin word *mores*, signifies morals. Since its object is not merely speculative knowledge, but the true direction of human acts, *Ethics* is also styled *Practical Philosophy*.

2. Ethics, we say, directs **human acts.** However, not all the acts of a man are called *human acts*, but only such as are under the control of his free will. Whatever he does necessarily—*i. e.*, whatever he cannot help doing—results from the physical laws of nature, and, as such, is willed and directed by the Author of nature. For instance, a man may fall like a stone, or grow like a plant, or perceive a sound like a brute animal, without any power on his part to prevent himself from falling or growing or hearing, if the required conditions are present. These are *acts of the man*, but they are not acts of what is distinctively human—namely, his intellect and his will. The term *human act* is restricted in Philosophy to those acts which a man does knowingly and willingly—which he has the power either to do or not to do.

3. To be qualified for the direction of human acts, Philosophy must derive its conclusions by reasoning from first principles; it must take into account the nature of man, and the natures of all the causes that influence human action.

Much of this we have considered in Metaphysics, or Mental Philosophy. **Ethics is thus founded on Metaphysics:** Moral Philosophy assumes as its principles the conclusions established in Mental Philosophy.

4. To explain the object of Moral Philosophy, which we have declared to be the true direction of human acts, we shall treat in Book I. *of the direction of human acts in general;* in Book II., *of the special duties and rights of men viewed as individuals;* and, in Book III., *of the rights and duties of men viewed as members of society.*

BOOK I.

THE DIRECTION OF HUMAN ACTS IN GENERAL.

5. In order to treat of the true direction of human acts, we shall examine in Chapter I. *the end or term to which such acts are to be directed;* in Chapter II., *the morality of human acts;* and, in Chapter III., *the rule by which they are to be directed to their end.*

CHAPTER I.

THE END TO WHICH HUMAN ACTS ARE TO BE DIRECTED.

In the present chapter we shall consider: 1. *Ends in general.* 2. *Our last end.* 3. *The attainment of our last end.*

Article I. Ends in General.

6. We mean here by **end** the purpose for which a thing exists; the end of an act is the purpose for which that act is done. For instance, some may read a certain book for pleasure; others for instruction, others again to practise obedience: the act is the same, the ends are various.

7. **Every human act is done for an end.** For a human act is an act of the will, and the will cannot act unless the intellect proposes to it something to which it may tend, *i. e.*, something good. The *will* is only another name for the *rational appetite*—that is, the power of tending to a good which the intellect proposes to it. The good intended is the end of the act. Hence, every act is done for an end. You may object that you have no special intention, *e. g.*, in reading; that you read merely to kill time, to be busied with something, etc.; nevertheless, you act for an end or purpose, the end in this case being to kill time or to find occupation.

8. We do not say that the end intended is always a *true* good, but only that it is always good after a manner; that it is

at least an **apparent good**, and aimed at because apprehended as good. It may be conceived as good in itself, worth tending to for its own sake, or as a means conducive to some other good. No man, however, intends evil for the sake of evil, but only because he sees something good and desirable in what he wills or in its result. A man may do evil to another for the sake of revenge, and thus do what is morally bad; he may do evil to himself—he may even kill himself; yet he cannot do so except for a purpose which he apprehends as good in some respect—for example, to be freed from trouble. No will can possibly act without aiming at something that has been apprehended as in some way desirable.

9. We must distinguish the **nearest** or proximate end, the **farther** or remote end, and the **last** or ultimate end, beyond which the agent does not look and in which his desire rests. Thus a student may exert himself in order to win a prize, because, by gaining the prize, he will please his parents, and by striving to please his parents he will please God. In this act of the student the prize is the *nearest* end, his parents *a farther* end, and God the *last* end.

Perhaps he does not think of God, but aims at pleasing his parents so as to receive a promised sum of money, with which finally he intends to buy some sweetmeats for the gratification of his palate. In this act he makes the enjoyment he derives from the gratification of his palate the last end.

10. In the example just given, the sweetmeats constitute the *objective* end; the enjoyment of them is the student's *subjective* end. The **objective** or **material** end is the object aimed at; the **subjective** or **formal** end is the attainment of that object.

11. We must also distinguish *the end of the work* from *the end of the workman*. A watchmaker, *e. g.*, constructs watches

in order to earn a living. **The end of the work,** the watch, is to mark the time; **the end of the workman** is to earn a living.

12. An end is said to be (a) **actually** intended, if at the time of the act it is thought of and aimed at; (b) **virtually** intended, if the act is influenced by a former intention to attain an end, though that end is not thought of at the time of the act; (c) **habitually** intended, if a former intention has not been retracted, yet does not for the time being affect the act; (d) **interpretatively** intended, if the act was not really intended, but would have been so intended, if the case in hand had been foreseen. Let us take an example. A boy is sent by his father to assist a distressed family. He sets out with the *actual* intention of fulfilling this commission. While walking along, he is occupied with other thoughts and is unmindful of his message, yet he directs his steps aright in virtue of his former intention—that is, with a *virtual* intention. He may delay for hours at a friend's house, totally uninfluenced by the purpose for which he started out; nevertheless, as that purpose has not been given up, it remains as a habit; it is *habitual*. At last he reaches the distressed family, and finds them in such want that he feels confident that his father, if he knew the circumstances, would wish him to give a larger alms than the sum appointed. Accordingly he gives this larger alms, acting on his father's intention as he interprets it. This is the father's *interpretative* intention—*i. e.*, what he would have actually intended if he had known the facts.

ARTICLE II. THE LAST END.

13. The last end, as stated above (No. 9), is that object in which the agent's desire rests. If in his act the agent excludes all reference to any further end, the end is **positively**

last; if such exclusion is not made, the end is **negatively** last. By the **absolutely last** end we mean that object which, by its very nature, requires that all action be subordinated to it, and that in it all desires shall rest.

14. The first principle of Moral Philosophy is this:

Thesis I. *God is the absolutely last end of all things.*

Proof. Such an end we have defined to be an object which, by its very nature, requires that all action be subordinated to it, and that in it all desires shall rest. Now God alone can be that object. For all things except God are contingent or unnecessary, *i. e.*, they have not in themselves the principle of their own existence (Ment. Phil. No. 104), but they exist only because and in so far as God gives them being (Ment. Phil. No. 220), and preserves them by His will and power (No. 263). Hence God possesses entire and perfect dominion over all things, and in the creature there is nothing that is not dependent on God. He has therefore the right to make all things tend to Himself and to rest in Him as in their last end. Moreover, He is bound to do so by His own perfections. For, since He is infinitely wise (Ment. Phil. No. 253), He must direct all things to an end worthy of Himself. Now, God alone is worthy of God. Consequently, God must require that all things tend ultimately towards Himself, and that in Himself all desires shall rest. Therefore God *is* the last end of all things.

15. But *how* do all things tend ultimately to God? We affirm that they must tend towards Him **with their whole being**; because God has made their whole being, the essence and the attributes of each, and all their powers. Now whatsoever He makes, He must direct ultimately to Himself as being the only end worthy of His action. Therefore all things must tend towards God with their whole being.

16. The direction which God gives to things is not a momentary extrinsic impulse, such, *e. g.*, as a musket-ball gets from the exploding powder; nor simply a continued extrinsic management, such as the leading of a horse by the bridle; but it is **an impulse intrinsic to every creature**, which is not distinct in reality from its very essence or nature and its peculiar tendencies. Hence, every action that the creature performs in accordance with its nature is towards that end for which it was created, namely, towards God Himself.

17. Of course, we do not say that every being tends **immediately** towards God. This can be said of intelligent beings only; yet all other beings tend **mediately** towards Him.

There is a broad truth in the saying, "Order is Heaven's first law." God's direction, which cannot fail to be wise, is ever appropriate to the nature of the thing directed. Hence, everything is so constituted as to tend towards that which is suited to its nature and is for its good; plants perform just those actions which are good for them, and this their own nature makes them do. By so acting they elaborate from the inert clod food for the animal kingdom. Animals perceive by their senses what is good for them, and are led by their appetites to appropriate that good. Man, finally, whom all material things subserve, tends by the faculties peculiar to himself, his intellect and will, to the knowledge and love of God, and is fitted and prompted by his rational nature to direct the material creation to the glory and service of his sovereign Lord.

18. As the inert clod supports vegetable life, as the vegetable is for the animal, and as the brute animal, together with all inferior things, is for man; so in man himself the lower powers are to subserve the higher powers, which are his intellect and will. Though each faculty has its own specific tendency to

its own specific good, still man is not a bundle of independent faculties; but he is a person, essentially one, fitted by nature to employ his faculties for the attainment of what is good for him in his specific nature as man. If, therefore, as it often happens, an inferior faculty craves what hinders rather than promotes the proper action of a higher faculty, reason then requires that such a craving be suppressed, in accordance with this principle of order: **the lower faculties are to be controlled by the higher.** The good craved in this case is not a real good for the person, but rather a real evil (Ment. Phil. No. 44). The intellect and will, when perfectly controlling the inferior faculties, are in a fit condition to follow up their own specific tendencies toward their proper objects, which are truth and all good worthy of man.

19. Good worthy of man is called **becoming, fit** or **proper.** In its strict meaning it is **moral good**—that good, namely, which is conformable to reason regulating free acts; in a wider meaning, it includes natural or physical good—that is, whatever perfects the nature of man, as health, knowledge, etc. Good viewed as conducive to the attainment of another good is styled **useful**; viewed as capable of giving satisfaction or pleasure to an appetite it is named **pleasurable.** The useful and pleasurable, when they are embraced by the will according to the right order of things and in a manner worthy of man, share in the nobility of moral good. Thus the pleasure which a dutiful son finds in making his parents comfortable and happy is morally good; and all the just and indifferent means used to promote this end are in the right order of human acts, and are therefore morally good.

20. Since God is the last end of all things (No. 14), He is, therefore, the last end of our highest powers, the intellect and will. But there is this **difference** between the tendencies of

our higher powers and the tendencies of other things: that, while the latter tend to God only *mediately*, our intellect and will tend to Him *immediately*, and do not find rest until they repose in Him as in their last end. When a brute animal has eaten and drunk what its appetite craves, it rests in the satisfaction of its animal desires, and longs for nothing beyond this. But our understanding and will can find rest in nothing short of the knowledge and love of God.

21. **Thesis II.** *By our intellect and will we must tend to God as our last end.*

Explanation. Of course, we do not say that it is wrong for man to love created things; but right order requires that we should make all these so many stepping-stones, as it were, to the higher plane of the knowledge and love of God. In this proposition, then, we maintain that the last end of man's intellect and will, that, namely, for which these faculties were given to him, is to know and to love God. We can prove this proposition in two ways: first, by considering the matter in the light of God's nature; and, secondly, by considering it from the standpoint of man's nature. However, we shall confine ourselves at present to the first consideration, which demonstrates that God is the objective end of man's highest powers; the second aspect we shall present further on in connection with man's subjective end (No. 32).

Proof. God is the absolute ultimate end (Thesis I.), the Supreme Good to which man is bound to tend. This tendency must be through faculties or activities by which he can apprehend the Supreme Good. He cannot do so by any organic faculty, because God is a pure spirit, and, consequently, not the object of organic perception. It must, therefore, be through his immaterial faculties, the spiritual activities of his soul, his intellect and will. Man's intellect, by its nature, is able to know God, and his will is able to love what the intellect knows and proposes as worthy of love. Therefore, by our intellect and will we must tend to God as our last end.

22. **Thesis III.** *God created all things for His own extrinsic glory.*

Explanation. Honor is the recognition of worth; when expressed in words, it is called *praise.* Glory is the praise of exalted merit, and in its full acceptance implies love as well as knowledge, together with the manifestation of the same by many persons as a tribute of homage that is due to the person glorified. The knowledge and love which God possesses with regard to Himself is His *intrinsic glory;* the homage of praise and love that creation renders to God is His *extrinsic glory.*

Proof 1. We have seen that God is the absolute ultimate end of all things; or, in other words, that all things must tend to Him as to their last end. Since this tendency is something willed by God, it is something good. Yet no good can be added to God intrinsically, because He is Himself the Infinite Good: it can, therefore, be added to God only extrinsically. God has no need of any extrinsic good; yet, if He creates at all, He must necessarily require that creatures shall proclaim Him as their Creator, and thus render Him the glory which is His due. Hence, the end God had in creating all things was His own extrinsic glory.

Proof 2. Man in particular, we know from thesis II., is bound to tend to the Supreme Good, his last end, by his intellect and will—that is, by knowing and loving God; but in these very acts of man consists the extrinsic glory of God. Therefore, man in particular was created for the extrinsic glory of God.

Objections.

1. Irrational creatures cannot praise and love God. *Answer.* They cannot love God, it is true; nor can they praise Him directly: nevertheless, they praise Him indirectly, by displaying God's power, goodness, wisdom, beauty, etc., to the intelligent creation, thereby serving to inspire and increase the praise and love of God on the part of man.

2. God cannot fail of His purpose, but He fails to receive the praise and love of the wicked. Therefore, He did not create them for that end. *Answer.* Though the wicked refuse God the homage of their love and voluntary praise in this life, they still serve to proclaim His praise. For in the next life they glorify His justice by their punishment, and even in the present life they make manifest His mercy and longanimity.

3. It would be unworthy of God to promote His glory by the misery of His creatures. *Answer.* To create man for misery would be unworthy of God, yes; we are maintaining that God, on the contrary, created all men for happiness, but on the condition that they shall render Him due service. When the wicked voluntarily turn away from their destined bliss by refusing to do their duty, they must necessarily incur a just punishment. The solution of this and similar difficulties will be better understood after we have treated of the sanction of the natural law (No. 107 et seq.).

24. As we remarked above (No. 10), the object aimed at or intended is the *objective* or *material end*, and the attainment or enjoyment of the object is the *subjective* or *formal end*. So

far we have proved that God is the objective end of all things, and particularly so of His rational creatures; we have explained, also, the manner in which all things tend to God by fulfilling the purpose which He had in view when creating them. We shall next consider the **subjective end of man**, *i. e.*, his attainment of his objective end.

ARTICLE III. THE ATTAINMENT OF OUR LAST END.

25. A man can labor for very different objects—now for honor, now for wealth, again for the pleasure of eating or drinking, or for the performance of duty, etc. Yet there is one thing common to all his objects, or ends, or purposes— namely, a desire of well-being, of happiness. **All men desire happiness,** but they often differ widely concerning the object in which they expect to find their happiness.

"Oh, happiness, our being's end and aim!
Good, pleasure, ease, content,—whate'er thy name."

26. Not only do all men desire happiness, but they also desire perfect happiness or beatitude. **Beatitude** may be defined as that state in which man is made perfect by the possession of all good things. It implies endless duration and the full satisfaction of all desires. Is such a state attainable by every man?

27. **Thesis IV.** *Every man can attain perfect happiness.*

Proof. If a certain good is found in all men, it must be part of man's nature, and hence it proceeds from the Author of nature. Now, there exists in us all, as we know by our consciousness, a desire of perfect happiness; and this desire is good, for by it we are impelled to perfect ourselves. Therefore, this desire proceeds from the Author of nature. But

God could not have implanted such a desire in our nature unless he gave us the means to satisfy it; because to allure us by a desire and a hope which He had destined to disappointment would be opposed to God's infinite goodness and truthfulness. Consequently, God has given us the means whereby every one of us can attain perfect happiness.

28. But here a difficulty presents itself. We often experience contradictory desires; a man, *e. g.*, may love peace, yet when provoked by an insult he feels inclined to break the peace. It is evident that perfect happiness cannot exist where desires are in conflict. How, then, can the conflict be made to cease? Clearly, not until the lower cravings of our complex nature cease to war against reason. But as this never comes to pass fully in this life, the logical inference is that **beatitude is not attainable in this life**. Yet we have proved it to be attainable; it follows, therefore, that we can gain perfect happiness in a future life.

29. At this point another question arises: Is man to be made supremely happy by being deprived of half his nature? Shall the soul be beatified alone, and the body moulder into dust? You may reply, there will be a **resurrection** by which all things will be made right. In that event, full gratification will be given to man's desires, among which there will never more be strife; for the faculties of his lower nature will be in perfect subjection to the spirit. This is the answer of Father Costa-Rossetti, S.J. and others, who maintain that in a purely natural order of things the soul cannot attain beatitude without the body. In the state of separation, they say, the soul would feel a longing to be reunited to the body, which nature intended for it, and with which it formed one person. Nothing prevents us, they continue, from supposing that a future resurrection belongs to the order of

nature, in this sense: that, as God gave us a natural desire for perfect happiness, He thereby pledged Himself to procure the realization of that desire for those who obey the laws of nature.

30. Most philosophers, however, consider the resurrection as entirely supernatural, and in no sense due to our nature, and they maintain that the soul can be **perfectly happy without the body.** To prove this point, they reason thus: The lower powers of man exist to subserve his higher powers in this life. When the soul possesses in the next life the full knowledge and love of God, it no longer needs the body or the lower faculties, and consequently it will have no desire for reunion with its inferior companion.

The authorities and arguments for both opinions are sufficiently weighty to warrant the student freedom to accept either. Whichever opinion be adopted, every objection against the attainment of beatitude can be satisfactorily answered.

31. **Thesis V.** *No created object can make man perfectly happy.*

Proof. Man is distinctively man chiefly by his intellect and will; hence no object can make him perfectly happy, unless it fully satisfies his intellect and will. This, however, no created object can do. Such objects are riches, honors, pleasures, human science and virtue. But as none of these, nor all of them together, can satisfy man's intellect and will, it is clear that no created object can make man perfectly happy.

> 1. *Not riches,* which are only a means of providing other good things. At their best they cannot last beyond the present life, and they do not perfect the intellect and will.

2. *Not honor.* For honor, whether viewed as the esteem which others have of us or as the outward manifestation of this esteem, cannot perfect our intellect and will. It generally has uncertain existence when it is obtained, and it cannot be obtained by all. Besides, honors are often bestowed upon the undeserving and denied to those who are most worthy of them.

3. *Not sensual pleasures*, which certainly cannot perfect our higher faculties. On the contrary, the pursuit of sensuality degrades man to the level of the brute; and surely it is absurd to say that man's perfect happiness consists in self-degradation.

4. *Not the human sciences.* Since human nature is essentially the same in all men, the perfect happiness of the human species must be the same in kind for every individual, and hence within the reach of all. But science is not within the reach of all, because many persons have not sufficient ability to acquire it. Being, moreover, something finite, science can neither satisfy the intellect, which is always reaching out for unlimited knowledge, nor the heart, which is capable of loving and, therefore, desiring the Infinite.

5. *Not virtue*, which consists in a habitual tendency to perfection. Virtue is consequently not the ultimate object of desire, but only a means to attain that object (No. 72 et seq.).

6. *Not all these united.* For they are all confined to the present life, and they cannot satisfy the desires of a being that longs for everlasting happiness.

32. **Thesis VI.** *God is the only object that can make man perfectly happy.*

Proof 1. Every man can attain perfect happiness (Thesis

IV.); therefore an object must be attainable that can make every man perfectly happy. But no created object can do this (Thesis V.). Therefore the Creator is the only object that can make man perfectly happy.

Proof 2. Man's perfect happiness supposes perfect satisfaction for his highest powers—*i. e.*, his intellect and will; but no object can give such satisfaction to these two powers except perfect truth and perfect goodness. For his intellect ever seeks to know the causes of things and the causes of these causes; nor can it ever rest content until it understands the First Cause. As the First Cause contains all good, the human will cannot help loving and desiring it when it is once known. Therefore the perfect or infinite truth and goodness, which is God, is the only object that can make man perfectly happy; in other words, the possession of God is our subjective last end.

33. Man's ultimate beatitude, as Philosophy treats it, viewing the subject by the light of reason alone, does not include the intuitive knowledge of God, the **beatific vision**, which we know from revelation to be really in store for us. The beatific vision is not due naturally to man or to any other creature; it is a supernatural gift. A soul in a state of natural beatitude would know God in a manner proportionate to its nature; it would understand the perfections of the Creator by reasoning from the knowledge it possesses of itself and other creatures. This knowledge of God, though abstract and not intuitive, would not be a cold speculation; on the contrary, in such a knowledge of a Being all good, all beautiful, all amiable, the soul would enjoy all perfection. Thus the primary element in natural beatitude would be the perfect knowledge of a perfect object. Yet, consequent on that knowledge and inseparable from it, as an attribute or even an

essential part of perfect happiness, would be the love and enjoyment of that object on the part of the will.

34. No one pretends that perfect happiness, as here described, can be attained in this life. The **nearest approach to it possible on earth** lies in the right ordering of our faculties towards the attainment of our last end. Indeed, from the nature of things and from the laws of harmony which an all-wise Creator has established in the universe, the happiness of a being is proportionate to that being's perfection. Hence the more perfect we become, the happier we shall be.

35. Moreover, we may distinguish three kinds of perfection; (a) *Physical* perfection, which supposes the possession of all the faculties required for the "acts of the man;" (b) *Moral* perfection, which regards our human acts as properly directed to our last end; (c) *Final* perfection, which consists in our attainment of that end. Possessing then the physical perfection of human nature, we must, to attain higher moral perfection, so order our faculties by the practice of virtue, that:

> 1. *Our lower powers* shall aid and never impede the proper action of the intellect and will. This implies that we must restrain and control our passions, and suppress all inordinate desires for bodily pleasures, riches, honors, and power. By so doing we shall live free from contention, impatience, restless ambition; from intemperance and lust, with their attendant degradation of body and soul.
>
> 2. *Our higher powers*, the intellect and will, shall tend to ennobling objects which bring us nearer to God. We ought to study His perfections. We should endeavor to appreciate His constant care for us, and to understand His supreme right to manage the whole course

of our lives. In this way we shall acquire an humble resignation to God's sovereign will, and a loving trust in His fatherly providence—dispositions which secure us in peace against the passing ills of life. Thus, unlike the Stoics of old, who vainly strove to imagine that there were no ills for the just on earth, we must accept, as men of sound common sense, the sufferings of this time in confidence and love, as purifications through which we are to pass to the full possession of eternal happiness in God.

3. *Of the goods of earth*, which are needed for our bodily life, we shall exert ourselves to obtain a sufficiency. Accordingly, a man should from his youth qualify himself for some respectable pursuit, in order either to procure a decent support for himself and those depending on him, or, if he already has the gifts of fortune, to enable him to pass successfully through possible reverses. With such an equipment, though his station in life may seem ever so lowly, a man can enjoy deeper peace of soul and greater happiness than those who abound in riches and honors and the world's false delights.

CHAPTER II.

THE MORALITY OF HUMAN ACTS.

36. Having discussed in the preceding chapter the end of human acts, we shall next proceed to study their nature. With this purpose we shall examine: 1. *The essential difference between morally good and morally bad acts, or the essence of morality;* 2. *The determinants of morality in any given action;* 3. *Accountability for moral acts;* 4. *Circumstances that lessen accountability;* 5. *The passions as influencing accountability;* 6. *Habits as facilitating moral acts.*

ARTICLE I. THE ESSENCE OF MORALITY.

37. Human acts are those of which a man is master, which he has the power of doing or not doing as he pleases. (No. 2. See also Ment. Phil., Nos. 194–199.) True, we are *physically* free to perform certain acts or to omit them—to do one thing or its contrary, to choose this act rather than some other; but are we also *morally* free in regard to all such acts? Is it right for me on all occasions to do whatever my inclination prompts me to do? My reason plainly answers, No: it is evident even to a child that some actions are good in themselves, *morally good*, and others bad in themselves, *morally bad*. The good acts our reason commends and approves; these we call *right*. Evil acts, on the contrary, our reason disapproves and blames; these we call *wrong*. The ideas of

right and *wrong*, like those of *truth* and *falsity, substance* and *accident, cause* and *effect* are " primary ideas " which are common to all men ; hence, they are trustworthy ideas—that is, the distinction existing in the mind between right and wrong corresponds to a distinction existing objectively in human acts. (See Logic, Nos. 119, 120.)

38. But though all men distinguish between right and wrong, it does not follow that all theorizers acknowledge the distinction. It often stands in the way of their **false speculations.** Such writers, for instance as Huxley, Spencer and the Agnostics and Positivists generally, admit no true liberty in man, and therefore they cannot consistently treat of human acts as such: there are no human acts with them, for there are no acts which a man has the power to do or not to do. The same holds true for all Materialists, who teach that nothing exists but matter—acting, of course, by necessary laws. Pantheists likewise, admitting no real distinction between man and God, cannot speak of human acts as such, and cannot therefore correctly explain the difference between moral right and moral wrong. Nevertheless, all these false theorizers employ the terms " right " and " wrong "—the distinction being too widely accepted to be ignored. They are forced, however, by the exigencies of their theories to misinterpret the meaning of these words. Without stopping to refute their false and demoralizing interpretations singly, we shall briefly explain the obvious, certain and common-sense distinctions between moral right and moral wrong.

39. **The reason why our intellect approves certain acts,** calls them *morally good* and pronounces them worthy of praise, precisely as free acts, is because it perceives that they are rightly directed to their true end, suitable to and worthy of a rational agent, conformable to the exigencies of things, and

therefore that they ought to be done by man: man *ought to do* what is conformable to his rational nature and conducive to his perfection.

Our intellect disapproves of other acts, calls them *morally bad* or *evil* and pronounces them to be, inasmuch as they are free acts, deserving of blame, because it perceives they are directed away from their true end, are unbecoming and unsuitable to a rational agent, at variance with the exigencies of things, and therefore not to be done by man: man *ought not to do* that which is unworthy of a rational being, and which, instead of perfecting, debases him.

40. **The radical notion conveyed by the term "good"** is "suitableness to an appetite or desire." Using the word, then, in its radical meaning, we say something is good for a being which that being desires—*i. e.*, which is the object of its appetites. And the good is the object of the being's appetites because it tends in some manner to the perfection of the being; for the wise Creator has made all things such that they tend to what promotes their perfection. Hence we call that a *physical good* which contributes to perfect a being physically—as, for example, food for the animal nature. We call whatever benefits the intellect, *e. g.*, truth and science, an *intellectual good*. So, too, that which perfects a free being, as such, we call a *moral good*.

41. A free being perfects itself by drawing near to its ultimate end, its supreme good, which is God. Consequently, those acts are morally good for man which bring him **nearer to God,** the ultimate end of his existence; and those are morally bad which lead him **away from God.**

42. Since there are some human acts, like blasphemy, that are of themselves bad at all times, and others, like reverence for God, that are of themselves always good, the quality of

goodness or badness must be something intrinsic to the acts and must depend upon their accord with or disagreement from the permanent natural order of things. It is clear that this order, with respect to human acts, corresponds to the relations which man, as a creature, possesses necessarily towards God; as a social entity, towards his fellow-men; and towards himself as a being endowed with various faculties, sensitive and spiritual. These relations in turn are founded on the essences of things; hence, the difference between the two classes of acts is an **essential difference.** Now the essences of things are modelled by the Creator upon perfections known to the Divine Intellect as existing in the Divine Essence; therefore the morality or immorality of a human act is determined ultimately by the intellect and not by the free will of God. As God can not contradict Himself, He can not make an intrinsically moral act immoral, nor remove the immorality of an act intrinsically immoral.

43. Some human acts are so disorderly as to turn a man entirely away from the pursuit of his true last end; for, in place of God as the ultimate object of desire, these acts substitute explicitly or implicitly something altogether incompatible with the love of God. There are other human acts, which, though impeding the soul's tendency towards its true ultimate end, do not become an obstacle to the attainment of that end. In this difference lies the distinction between **mortal** and **venial sin.**

44. Once the true meaning of morality is grasped, it is easy to detect the errors of certain **false theories** which have been fabricated to explain the power residing in all men of distinguishing between good and evil.

1. Some philosophers attribute this power to *instinct.*

But instinct, in the accurate meaning of the word, is

a blind impulse of nature, which prompts the animal to conduct itself in a determined manner, and thus to perform complex acts, without understanding their further purpose, for the good of the individual and of the species. Moral good and moral evil, on the contrary, are apprehended intellectually—that is, by a cognitive faculty which can reflect and draw inferences; hence, in distinguishing between good and evil, we do not act blindly, but intelligently.

2. Some speak of a *moral sense.* If by a moral sense an organic faculty or the action of an organic faculty is meant, the use of the term is erroneous and misleading; because material organism, which is required for every organic action, cannot possibly grasp the abstract immaterial relations contained in the idea of moral good or evil. If, however, the term is employed to denote a certain perfection of the intellectual powers, a quickness and keenness of mind in detecting and judging the morality or immorality of human acts, it is used correctly.

3. Others maintain with Herbert Spencer[*] that this power of distinguishing between good and evil rests upon the power of distinguishing between what is *useful* and what is *hurtful* to men generally in the present life. Whatever tends to the temporal good of mankind generally is morally good, they say, and whatever generally does injury is morally evil. Now,

---

[*] I believe that the experiences of utility organized and consolidated through all past generations of the human race have been producing corresponding modifications, which, by continued transmission and accumulation, have become in us certain faculties of moral intuition, certain emotions corresponding to right and wrong conduct, which have no apparent basis in the individual experiences of utility. (*Spencer's Letter to Mill.*)

it is true that moral good is ultimately useful to mankind even on earth, and moral evil is ultimately injurious. But moral good is not good because it is useful; on the contrary, it is useful because it is good, *i. e.*, because it tends to make man more perfect, and hence better fitted to attain his last end. Moreover, it is a part of the universal harmony which God has established in His creation, that the moral good of the individual be either immediately or ultimately beneficial to the many. In this sense, honesty is truly the best policy.

4. In the theories of Hobbes, Paley, Mandeville, and the older English Utilitarians, regard to *personal* advantage on earth is the only motive of human action: that is morally good which brings me pleasure; the "moral good" is the "useful to me personally."

5. Finally, some in theory and very many in practice hold that the *norma* or rule of right and wrong lies in the *opinion of men*. That is right, they declare, which the majority of men approve. "*Vox populi, vox Dei*"— "The voice of the people is the voice of God." But on many topics the opinions of men are changeful and often false. When, moreover, all men agree in calling a certain act good or evil, they do so because they see that in itself it is good or evil; but it is not good or evil because they call it so.

45. It may be asked **whether every human act is either good or evil.** We must make a distinction.

1. An act considered in the abstract, *i. e.*, apart from all circumstances, may be specifically neither good nor evil. For instance, walking, riding, reading, etc., are

acts that in themselves do not imply a tendency to our last end or a departure from it. All such are called *indifferent acts:* specifically, they are neither good nor bad.

2. But every moral act considered *individually, i. e.*, as done in such and such circumstances of time, place and persons, is necessarily either good or bad. For, since we distinguish a good from a bad act by its conformity with fixed principles known to reason, it follows that when reason approves, the act is right; when it disapproves, the act is wrong. Now, in every individual human act, reason approves the act as a fit object for a deliberate choice, or disapproves it as an unfit object for such choice; therefore, every individual or concrete human act is either right or wrong.

The truth of this principle is made clearer in the next article.

ARTICLE II. THE DETERMINANTS OF MORALITY.

46. To know whether an individual human act is morally good, we must consider it with reference to these three things which, because they determine the moral character of acts, are called the **determinants** of morality: 1st. The object of the act; 2d. The end, or purpose; 3d. Its circumstances. That the act may be morally good, all three determinants must be without a flaw, according to the received axiom: "*Bonum ex integra causa, malum ex quocumque defectu*,"—" A thing to be good must be wholly so; it is vitiated by any defect."

47. I. **The object** of an act is the thing done. In reality,

it is not distinct from the act itself; for we cannot act without doing something, and the something done is the object of the act; say, of going, eating, praising, etc. The act or object may be viewed as containing a further specification— *e. g.*, going to church, praising God, eating meat. Now, an act thus specified may, when considered in itself, be good, bad, or indifferent; thus, to praise God is good in itself, to blaspheme is bad in itself, and to eat meat is in itself an indifferent act. But that an individual act may be good, its object, whether considered in itself or as further specified, must be free from all defect; *it must be good, or at least indifferent.*

48. II. *The end*, or purpose, intended by the agent is the second determinant of an act's morality. The end here spoken of is not the end of the work, for that pertains to the object, but the end of the workman or agent (No. 11). No matter how good the object of an act may be, if the end intended is bad, the act is thereby vitiated. Thus, to praise God is good in itself, but, if in so acting the intention be to play the hypocrite, the act is morally bad. And this holds true whether the vicious end be the nearest, remote or last end (No. 9); whether it be actually or only virtually intended (No. 12). On the other hand, a good end, though ever so elevated, cannot justify a bad act; in other words, we are never allowed to do evil that good may result therefrom.*

49. *The circumstances* of time, place and persons have their part in determining the morality of an individual act. The moral character of an act may be so affected by attendant circumstances, that an act good in itself may be evil when

---

* The doctrine that the end justifies the means has been falsely attributed to the Catholic Church, and particularly to the Jesuits. No institutions in the world have more strenuously opposed the pernicious tenet either in their theory or their practice.

accompanied with certain circumstances; for instance, it is good to give drink to the thirsty, but if the thirsty man is morally weak, and the drink is intoxicating, the act may be evil.

50. Under the head of circumstances certain effects of an act may be included; not such effects as are directly willed or intended, for these go with the second class of determinants (No. 48). But there may be other effects which the agent foresees or can foresee so related to the act, that, though he does not intend them, yet he consents to their taking place, inasmuch as he wills the act which, to his knowledge, is the cause or at least the occasion of these effects. Thus, in ordering a city to be bombarded, a general brings about, however reluctantly, the death of many non-combatants. Such an effect, he is said to **permit**, or **to will indirectly.**

51. If besides the good effects directly intended in an act evil effects are foreseen as likely to result, the act is not licit unless it fulfills the following **conditions**: 1. That the evil effect be not directly intended; 2. That the good effect intended be not produced by means of the evil effect, for we are never allowed to do evil that good may come therefrom. The general in the foregoing example does not kill the non-combatants in order that *by their death* he may destroy the combatants; 3. That the good directly intended exceed the evil effects. No one could licitly bombard a city for the sake of a slight advantage; 4. That the doer of the act be not under the obligation of averting the evil consequences in question.

52. **The external action** commanded by the will derives its good or evil character from the internal, elicited act of the will; hence, outward action does not of itself increase the right or wrong of the act. Indirectly, however, it may

readily do so; because outward action is apt to protract or intensify the inward disposition of the will, and thus increase the moral good or evil of the act.

Article III. Accountability for Moral Acts.

53. When I perform a free act—one which I am able to do or not to do, as I choose—the act is evidently **imputable** to me: if the thing is blameworthy, the blame belongs to me; if it is praiseworthy, I am entitled to the praise. Every human act, therefore, since it is a free act (No. 2), is imputable to him who performs it.

54. But **am I accountable** for my free acts—and to whom? Is there any one who has the right and the power to hold me answerable for my moral conduct? So far, we have not touched upon this question. We have simply shown that some acts are morally good and some are morally bad; that some ought to be done, and others ought not to be done (No. 39); and we have examined into the distinction between these two classes of acts, or the nature of morality. Proceeding further, we are now to show that a Higher Will binds us to observe the moral law (which consists in doing what is right and avoiding what is wrong), and holds us accountable for our moral conduct—*i. e.*, for our observance of the moral law. The Higher Will, which imposes the moral law upon us, is none other than the Supreme Will of God.

55. God's right to bind us is clear from the fact that He is our Creator and we are His creatures. (Ment. Phil., No. 211 et seq.) Now that which is made out of nothing, or created, belongs entirely to its Creator; therefore we, His creatures, belong entirely to God, and consequently He has a perfect right to the homage and service of our whole being. In the following thesis we shall demonstrate the great truth that God requires of us the observance of the moral law. It would be absurd to say that such observance degrades man. One might say, just as reasonably, that subjection to the laws of civilization is degrading to a savage. Nor is this comparison farfetched, since the moral law is the central figure of civilized society.

56. **Thesis VII.** *God's will imposes the law of morality upon us, and holds us accountable for our observance of it.*

Proof 1. The Infinitely wise Creator cannot fail to employ the proper means to direct all things to their appointed ends; hence, He directs by necessary tendencies beings that are not endowed with free will. Over these tendencies such beings have no control: thus He directs matter by physical laws; brute animals by instincts. Free beings He must also direct in the manner proper to their nature, *i. e.*, requiring them to attain their appointed end by the *free choice* of the means peculiarly adapted to this object. Now, to require this of us, is to impose the law of morality upon us, since we tend towards our appointed end by doing what is right, and we fail to tend towards our end by doing what is wrong. Moreover, if the imposition of this law is to be effectual, as in His Infinite wisdom He is bound to make it, God must hold us accountable for our moral conduct. (See Ment. Phil., Nos. 222, 225.)

Proof 2. It is shown in Critical Logic (Nos. 156–164), that the judgments made by the common sense of mankind are true. Now, one of these judgments is that we are responsible for our moral acts to a Supreme Ruler, for this is found in the minds of all men who have the full use of reason; nor can a man rid himself of this conviction, though he may eagerly desire to do so. Therefore, all men are accountable for their moral conduct, *i. e.*, for their observance of the moral law, to God, who is the Supreme Ruler, as He is the Creator of all things.

57. To say that God holds us accountable for our free acts, implies that He will punish us if we do moral evil. We shall show presently that we become entitled to reward by doing what is morally good. A title to reward, on account of good actions, is called **merit**. The foundation of merit is this principle of reason, that *if a person freely benefits another, the latter ought, in equity, or by way of compensation, to make a proportionate return.*

58. Merit is of two kinds. **Condign merit** is a strict title to a reward, on account either of a promise freely given or of a benefit received; it, moreover, imposes an obligation upon one person to make an adequate return to another. **Congruous merit** is not a strict title to a recompense, but only a matter of propriety or suitableness in the bestowal of a reward; hence there is no just claim on the one side and, consequently, no real obligation on the other.

59. Condign merit demands the fulfillment of two **conditions**: 1. The benefit conferred must be in no way due to the recipient; we can claim no reward from another for paying him a debt. 2. The person benefited must accept explicitly or implicitly the service rendered, or, at least, he ought to accept it. If this condition were not required, I should be obliged to pay every tradesman that might choose to send me his wares.

60. **Thesis VIII.** *We can merit a reward from men, and from God also, though not in the same sense.*

Part I. *Merit with regard to our fellow-men. Proof.* We often have the power either to confer or not to confer a benefit upon our fellow-men, according as we choose. Now, if we freely do good to others, reason dictates that they ought to do good to us in return; and thus we have a title, founded on reason, to receive a reward from our fellow-men. This title is called merit. Hence we can merit a reward from men.

Part II. *Merit with regard to God. Proof.* We are often physically free either to do a certain act, whereby we honor God and thus contribute to His external glory, or not to do the act. If we perform the act in question, we give to Him what is, in some manner, a benefit, and we have what is, in some manner, a claim to receive a benefit in return.

Part III. *The latter is not merit in the same sense as our merit with men. Proof.* The good we do our fellow-men, in so far as it is not due to them, obliges them strictly to a proportionate return; but we cannot strictly give anything to God which is not entirely due to Him, since, as creatures, we belong in every way to God our Creator. Consequently, if He owes us a reward at all, it is not for the benefits He receives at our hands; but only because He owes it to Himself to fulfill His promises of a reward. For, by implanting in every heart an insatiable longing after perfect happiness, He has implicitly promised us a reward—on condition, of course, that we do our part. Therefore, we can merit a reward from God and men: from men, by reason of that which they owe us; from God, by reason of that which He owes Himself.

ARTICLE IV. HINDRANCES TO ACCOUNTABILITY.

61. Since our accountability for an act is based on our power to control the act, whatever hinders or lessens this power must, to the same extent, hinder or lessen our accountability. There are mainly four such **hindrances**: *ignorance, concupiscence, fear* and *violence.*

62. I. Ignorance is the absence of knowledge. In Ethics it regards two classes of objects—viz., laws and facts. If a man does not know that marriage between third cousins is forbidden, he is ignorant of the law. If he is not aware that his betrothed is his third cousin, he is ignorant of the fact. Ignorance, whether of the law or of the facts, is either *vincible* or *invincible*. When it cannot be overcome by the due amount of diligence, it is invincible; otherwise, it is vincible. The latter is said to be *gross* or *supine* when scarcely an effort has been made to remove it; and if a person deliberately avoids enlightenment in order to sin more freely, his ignorance is *affected*.

63. Thesis IX. *We are free from responsibility for acts performed through invincible ignorance, but not for acts done in ignorance that is vincible.*

Part I. *In cases of invincible ignorance, we are not responsible. Proof.* We are responsible for our acts only inasmuch as they are human acts. Now an act, inasmuch as it is done through invincible ignorance, is not a human act; for, in that respect, an essential element of a human act is wanting, namely, knowledge. Therefore we are not responsible for acts performed through invincible ignorance.

Part II. *Vincible ignorance does not free us from responsibility. Proof.* This ignorance could have been removed if we had so willed; hence, it is voluntary As any deordination in the act performed is caused by our voluntary ignorance, it becomes voluntary in its cause. But what is voluntary in its cause affects the morality of the act, as was explained above (Nos. 50, 51), and we are responsible for the morality of our acts. Therefore, vincible ignorance does not free us from responsibility.

64. Objections. 1. Invincible ignorance is rejected when offered as an excuse before civil tribunals. *Answer.* Human judges, unlike the Divine Judge, cannot see our thoughts. They are thus forced to consider presumptions of guilt, and it is presumed that a law duly promulgated is known to all.

2. In cases of invincible ignorance, our acts are free. Therefore we are accountable for them. *Answer.* Though free in other respects, they are not free violations of the law. For if I cannot know the law, I cannot will to violate it.

65. II. **Concupiscence** is a strong impulse of the sensible appetite inclining the will to seek sensible good and to fly from sensible evil. When it arises unbidden by the will, it is termed *antecedent;* but when it arises at the command, or continues with the consent, of the will, it is called *consequent.* As soon as sensible good or evil is perceived, the appetite generally acts instinctively. This first impulse is not free, and consequently not imputable to us. In as far as concupiscence impels the will, it restrains our liberty, and thus lessens our accountability. Yet, unless the impulse be so violent as to deprive us for the time being of the use of reason, it does not dispossess our will of the power to refuse consent; hence, when the will yields, though its consent may be reluctant, it does so freely and we are responsible. Consequent concupiscence is a willful intensification of consent, which therefore increases our responsibility.

66. III. **Fear** arises from the apprehension of threatening evil, and prompts us to seek safety in flight. Our will is thus dragged along, as it were, and so its freedom is restricted and our responsibility is diminished to the same extent. Great fear sometimes exempts a person from acts enjoined by positive law.

67. IV. Violence is an impulse from without tending to force the agent to act against his choice. It cannot affect the will directly—*i. e.*, the elicited acts of the will—for we cannot will that which at the same time we do not will. But violence can sometimes affect our external acts. In so far as the violence is irresistible, we are not responsible for the external act. If, however, the will yields a reluctant yet real consent, we are blamable, though in a lower degree than if there had been no reluctance.

Article V. The Passions.

68. We have just explained how the passions of concupiscence and fear may affect our responsibility. It will be useful at this stage to consider the passions in general, the various kinds, the nature of each, the purpose for which they exist, and the use we should make of them.

Passions are movements of the irrational part of the soul attended by a notable alteration of the body, on the apprehension of good or evil. In the strict meaning of the word, passions are *organic* affections aroused by *sensible* good or evil. As such, they are common to man and brute, but impossible in an angel. Nevertheless, the names of various passions are often used analogically to denote affections of the will, that are entirely, or at least chiefly, due to intellectual cognition, as when we are said to love science, to hate ignorance, to desire honor, to enjoy a joke, etc. To this latter class belong the *moral emotions*, such as admiration of virtue, detestation of vice, etc. Owing, indeed, to the substantial union of our soul and body, the one cannot be strongly affected without, as a general rule, reacting on the other. For both sensitive and intellectual knowledge are accompanied with phantasms, by means of which the sensitive and, indirectly, the rational appetites are aroused to action. Besides, in man there is really only one will; which is called *affective* to denote the impulse of the sense-faculty, and *elective* to denote the free choice of the rational faculty, and it scarcely ever acts powerfully in either faculty without acting also in the other.

69. **Our passions are of two kinds,** *concupiscible* and *irascible.*

1. The **concupiscible** passions are those affections of the sensible faculties which regard their object as simply good or evil. They are six in number: good or evil in general excites *love* or *hate* respectively; *desire* is roused by good apprehended as absent, *aversion* by an approaching evil; when the good is attained, *joy* is excited, whilst, on the other hand, present evil causes *sadness.*

2. The **irascible** passions, which are five in number, arise when good or evil is apprehended as associated with difficulties or obstacles to be overcome. Difficulty or even danger in connection with a desired good is not always displeasing. If the attainment of a desired good which is difficult to acquire is apprehended as within our power, *hope* is aroused; if it seems to be quite beyond our reach, *despondency* follows. In the case of a coming evil, we are animated by *courage* if we feel that we can avert it, but we experience *fear* on perceiving that we cannot easily escape. *Anger* is roused by the presence of an evil to which we are unwilling to submit (St. Thomas, I ma 2 æ, q. 23). These eleven may be called *the*

primary passions. All others are modifications or combinations of these.

70. The passions are intended by the Creator to assist us in attaining our last end. Hence in themselves **they are not evil, but good.** Yet they must be subject to the careful control of the will enlightened by reason. Generally their first impulses arise by a kind of physical necessity when the senses apprehend good or evil. However, as these first impulses are not free, they are not imputable to us. But as soon as the intellect perceives their presence, the will can act; and it must assert its control to regulate or suppress their movement, according as reason judges it to be right or wrong. If the will fails to do this, we become accountable for the consequences. The moral perfection of a man consists, to a great extent, in his power to control his passions and to direct their energies aright. Persevering efforts thus to regulate the passions beget good habits, which are invaluable aids for attaining our last end.

71. **Zeno and the Stoics** totally misconceived the relation of the passions to morality; they pronounced them to be moral disorders, which a virtuous man was bound to uproot from his heart. He was not to allow the sensitive appetite even to stir. Now, it is impossible to suppress all movement of passion; indeed, to check passion when it is conducive to true happiness, would be very unwise. It would make all impassioned eloquence and poetry impossible; it would cut off all high-spirited devotion to duty, all unselfish spontaneity, and banish generous pity and noble enthusiasm. The ideal of human nature fancied by the Stoics would be a mere calculating machine. A man's father and mother might be slain before his eyes, whilst he would be busy stifling his heart's natural impulse to fly to the rescue. The true doctrine which

we have here outlined was formulated by Aristotle and his followers, the Peripatetics; but in its stead the Stoics attempted to substitute their strange misconceptions of the truth.

Article VI. Virtues and Vices.

72. **Habits** are defined as more or less permanent qualities which dispose a faculty to act readily and with ease. A habit results naturally from frequent repetition of the same act. Thus, by constantly restraining the passion of anger, a person gains facility in doing so; or, in other words, he acquires the virtue of meekness. A habit is said to be "a second nature," because though not constituting nature it greatly facilitates certain operations of the natural faculties. Good habits, or those inclining us to do what is morally right, are called *virtues;* bad habits, or tendencies to what is wrong, are called *vices*. Brute animals are incapable of moral acts; hence they cannot form moral habits. Their power of imitation or the influence of peculiar circumstances may, it is true, enable them to acquire ways of acting which are not ordinary, which may indeed seem unnatural; as, when a bird is made to pronounce words. The power to act thus may be termed a habit, but, of course, not a moral habit. Man may also acquire habits that are more or less mechanical; but, besides these, he can form moral habits by the frequent repetition of free acts; and in Moral Philosophy we are concerned with only the latter class of habits.

73. Certain habits may be **supernaturally infused** into the soul, and in no other way can the supernatural virtues of Faith, Hope and Charity be obtained; so that natural acts, though ever so numerous, cannot of themselves produce a supernatural habit. Even natural virtues may be supernat-

urally infused or strengthened by Almighty God. Philosophy, however, considers only natural virtues and the natural mode of acquiring and developing them, all of which depend on the repetition of virtuous acts.

74. **Virtue and vice necessarily imply freedom of action;** no one is truly said to be virtuous for doing what he cannot help doing, nor can any one be called vicious for doing what he cannot possibly avoid. Now, freedom is a power belonging peculiarly to man's will; therefore all vices and virtues must, in some manner, be referred to the will. Besides, the will can influence the intellect considerably, not in regard to such judgments as are immediately evident, but in regard to the less immediate conclusions of reasoning. In this way it can so bend the intellect to consider certain motives for action to the exclusion of other motives that, after repeated acts of the same kind, the intellect finds great ease in certain modes of action rather than in others.

The will can also control the sensitive appetites or passions; and, as these are of two kinds, the concupiscible and the irascible, the relation of the passions to the will gives rise to two classes of virtues and vices. Accordingly, the moral virtues are reducible to four heads, called **the four cardinal virtues:** namely, _justice_, a habit belonging directly to the will; _prudence_, dwelling in the intellect; _temperance_, regulating the concupiscible passions, and _fortitude_, commanding the irascible passions.

75. I. **Justice** perfects the will, inclining it to choose always that which tends to our true good and the attainment of our last end. As such it is a general virtue, and includes all the virtues. In a more restricted sense, justice inclines us to give to every one his due—to God by the virtue of _religion_, to our parents by _filial piety_, to our benefactors by _gratitude_,

To other men we give their due by acts of what is commonly understood as *justice*. This, in turn, is of two kinds: *commutative justice*, by which we give to other men *quid pro quo*, *i.e.*, an exact equivalent in return for what they give us; *distributive justice*, a virtue of the ruler, by which he distributes the honors, rewards, burdens, etc., of the community according to the merits and conditions of his subjects.

76. II. **Prudence** perfects the intellect, directing it to discern on all occasions what is best suited for the attainment of our last end. Thus defined, prudence is a general virtue, which includes: (a) *Clear-sightedness*, or a quick, accurate perception of the true value of means to an end; (b) *Caution*, which bids us take time to notice difficulties and to provide against them; (c) *Self-distrust*, which disposes us to examine matters with care, and to accept the advice of others, especially if our own case is in question.

77. When clear-sightedness is perverted to the attaining of a morally bad end, it degenerates into the vice of *craftiness* or cunning; when carried to excess, caution becomes *timidity*, self-distrust turns into *pusillanimity*, and docility is changed into *simplicity*. In these, as in other matters, it is the part of prudence to indicate the *proper mean*, or middle course between excess and defect—" *virtus in medio*," "virtue holds the middle course"—the golden mean between too much and too little. "Avoid extremes" is an important maxim in moral conduct.

78. III. **Temperance** governs the sensible appetites in the use of things that especially attract them—namely, sensible pleasures. The will can restrain these appetites and accustom them to follow the guidance of reason. When this is brought about, they are said to be well ordered, and as such they contribute to man's perfection. The virtue of tem-

perance does not consist in an entire abstinence from what the sensible appetites crave, but rather in the golden mean of moderate use. A higher degree of restraint belongs to the virtue of *mortification*. Still, the golden mean of temperance cannot be kept perfectly without constant checks upon the cravings of the passions—that is, without sometimes practising mortification by denying ourselves allowable pleasures. Concupiscence is like a fiery horse, which must be early broken in and controlled ever afterwards with a firm hand.

79. IV. **Fortitude** is the virtue by which the will commands the irascible passions to attempt what is lofty, though the means are arduous and even perilous, and to bear evils with composure. It thus embraces *courage* and *patience*. To attempt what is lofty is *magnanimous;* to contemn difficulties in the way is *brave*. *Cowardice* is the absence of fortitude; but fortitude, when carried to excess, *i.e.*, beyond the bounds prescribed by prudence, grows into *rashness*. Thus, fortitude, like other virtues, must adhere to the golden mean. In this or that person, each of these four virtues may have different degrees of strength; nevertheless, no virtue can be perfect without the companionship of the others.

CHAPTER III.

LAW THE RULE OF HUMAN ACTS.

80. We have already proved (No. 56) that man is accountable to his Creator for his free acts; this, moreover, is a judgment of the common sense of mankind. Yet reason does not originate God's supreme control; it does not make the law. But it recognizes and reveals, as decreed by the sovereign will, a rule outside and independent of us, according to which our actions ought to be directed. Now, a rule directive of action is called a **law**, the word being used *in its widest sense*. Thus the laws of physical nature are rules in accordance with which the actions of material things are directed. *In a stricter sense*, the term "law" expresses the direction of free acts, and, as such, it is a rule directive of human acts. In this last meaning only, is the word "law" employed in Moral Philosophy.

Reason not only reveals to us the existence of certain general laws affecting human conduct, but it dictates their application to individual human acts. Viewed as a faculty thus directive of individual acts, reason is called *conscience*.

We shall consider in the present chapter: 1. *The moral law in general;* 2. *The application of the moral law by conscience;* 3. *The sanction of the moral law.*

ARTICLE I. THE MORAL LAW IN GENERAL.

81. A law, we have said, is "a rule directive of human acts." Still more explicitly defined, "**a law** is an ordinance of

reason which is for the common good, and has been promulgated by one having charge of the community." As doubt may sometimes arise whether a given enactment is really a law, and has the force of a law, a careful examination of every word in this definition is in order.

(a) A law is an *ordinance of reason;* it proceeds as an ordinance from the will of the law-giver, after it has originated in his intellect. He perceives a right course of action which is useful or necessary, and he wills to impose an obligation, on those who are subject to his decrees, to follow this course of action. Law is distinguished from mere counsel by the note of obligation. Still the law has no other binding force than the ruler intended.

(b) *For the common good.* A law is imposed on the general community, not on individuals, though it does not necessarily affect the actions of all individuals composing the community, but only certain classes, *e. g.*, merchants, lawyers, taxpayers, voters, etc. Nevertheless, the effect intended must redound to the common good.

(c) It is manifest that a law cannot be enacted except by the person, physical or moral, that has *charge of the whole community*. By his position, such a one is bound to direct all the members of the community to their common good; and as the enactment of laws is a necessary means to this end, he has the right—and he alone—of making laws.

(d) *Promulgation* is essential for the obligation of a law, so that, without this, even if the lawgiver should wish the immediate observance of an ordinance, there is no binding force. The reason is apparent. A law is directive of human acts; but without promulgation a law cannot be the subject of human acts, because an essential requisite, the knowledge needed for such an act, is wanting.

82. A law decreed by Almighty God is a *divine law;* one established by man is a *human law.* Those laws for human conduct which God, having once decreed creation, necessarily enacts in accordance with that decree, constitute the *natural law;* those which God or man freely enacts are *positive laws.* Now, between the natural law and positive laws, there are these **four points of difference:**

1. The natural law, unlike positive laws, does not depend upon the free will of God; its requirements flow from the intrinsic difference between right and wrong, which is determined by the very essences of things (No. 42). Hence, under this law, certain acts are not evil primarily because they are forbidden, but they are forbidden because in themselves they are evil.

2. Consequently, the natural law is the same at all times, in all places, and for all persons; but this is not true of positive laws, which may be changed with changing circumstances, or, if the law-giver so wills it, even without change of circumstances.

3. The natural law emanates from God alone; but positive laws may be enacted by men.

4. The natural law is promulgated through the light of reason; positive laws require for their promulgation a sign external to man.

83. As a consequence of the foregoing, **the natural law may be defined** as the ordinance of Divine Wisdom, which is made known to us by reason, and which requires the observance of the moral order. It may also be defined to be, "The eternal law as far as it is made known by human reason." By *the eternal law* we mean all that God necessarily decrees from eternity. That part of the eternal law,

which reason reveals as directive of human acts, we call the natural law.

84. **A universal formula** which contains in brief an expression of the whole natural law is this: " Keep the moral order," or "Observe right order in your actions." Some writers state it simply as, " Do good and avoid evil." Now, the right order of human acts consists evidently in their proper direction to man's last end, which is, subjectively, his perfect beatitude and, objectively, God Himself (Nos. 40, 41). God must direct His free creatures to their last end, hence He commands them to observe the moral order and forbids them to depart from it.

85. Consequently, **nothing can excuse us** from observing the moral law or any part of it, though such observance be attended with the most distressing difficulties, and demand from us the most heroic sacrifices—the sacrifice even of our lives.

86. We must note, however, that the **affirmative** precepts of the natural law differ, in respect to obligation, from the **negative** precepts. The latter, which forbid certain acts, always remain in force, so that the forbidden acts are never allowed. Thus no one is ever allowed to dishonor God; this negative precept holds always and for all persons. Affirmative precepts, or those commanding certain acts, oblige only for certain times or occasions; the affirmative precept to honor God does not oblige us to worship Him uninterruptedly.

87. By saying **the natural law is immutable**—*i.e.*, not susceptible of change (No. 82), we mean that an act morally bad by its nature cannot become morally good. Nor can any precept of the natural law be *abrogated*—*i. e.*, totally done away with; nor be *derogated from*, by partially losing its binding force; nor admit of *dispensation.*

Yet some acts indifferent in themselves, which derive their moral goodness or badness from attending circumstances, may seem to change their moral character. For example, during many ages capital was considered unproductive—*i. e.*, it did not fructify, it had no market value—and hence to exact even moderate interest for money lent was held to be unjust, because, in accordance with the economic practices of the period, this was a demand for a recompense not due. But with the change of times, the methods of business and commerce have changed, so that now capital has a market value, and is said to fructify. Consequently, it is everywhere considered to be a productive article, for the use of which it is just and lawful to require a fair recompense.

88. **Thesis X.** *The natural law is eternal and unchangeable.*

Proof. All men have, at all times, the same essence, or nature; hence they have the same ultimate end, and the same natural means necessary for attaining that end. These means the omniscient Creator knew and decreed from eternity, and therefore, by an eternal act of His will, He requires for all times the employment of these means. Now, the natural means necessary for man's attainment of his last end consists in his observance of the natural law, which is consequently eternal as a divine decree, and unchangeable with the unchangeableness of man's nature.

89. **Objections.** 1. God allowed the Israelites when they were leaving Egypt to steal the silver and gold of the Egyptians (Exod. xii.), yet theft is against the natural law. *Answer.* Granting, for the sake of argument, that this is the correct interpretation of the passage cited, we deny that such a permission would be

against the natural law. Theft is the appropriation of what belongs to another without or against the latter's will. Now all possessions belong absolutely to God, and He has the absolute right to dispose of them. If, then, the Israelites received from God express permission to appropriate certain goods belonging to their oppressors, even against the will of the latter, they did not commit theft, since they had the full consent of the absolute Owner.

2. God commanded Abraham to kill an innocent person, and murder is surely opposed to the natural law. *Answer.* The killing of an innocent person by private authority is plainly opposed to the natural law. But God is the supreme Lord of life, and therefore He can deprive His creatures of life when He sees fit, and in the manner He chooses, whether directly or indirectly—*i. e.*, by the ministry of angels, of men, or of other creatures.

90. Though the natural law is made known to us by our reason, it does not follow that every person on attaining the full use of reason acquires a complete knowledge of the law. Philosophers divide its precepts into **three classes**: 1. The fundamental principles immediately expressed by the universal formula, "Keep the moral order," or "Do good and avoid evil." 2. Obvious consequences drawn directly from the fundamental principles, which are applied to particular classes of acts; to these belong the precepts of the Decalogue, with the exception of the third. 3. More remote conclusions drawn from the fundamental principles by rather intricate processes of reasoning.

91. **Thesis XI.** *The natural law in its most general principles and their immediate applications, i. e., the first and*

second classes of its precepts, cannot be invincibly unknown by those who have the full use of reason.

Proof 1. God cannot, in His goodness and wisdom, leave a man without the means necessary to attain his last end; but the knowledge of the natural law in its most general principles and their immediate application is a necessary means to this end for all men that have the full use of reason. Therefore, God cannot leave such men without this knowledge or at least the opportunity to acquire it.

Proof 2. The thesis is made evident by investigating the nature of the precepts contained in the two classes specified. Those of the first class are first principles in the moral order and, like the first principles of the speculative order, are admitted to be self-evident. The precepts of the second class forbid acts which in themselves are evil, and enjoin acts which in themselves are good and directly necessary for the attainment of man's last end. These latter precepts flow from the first principles of the moral order by inference so easy that the rudest minds are capable of performing the necessary reasoning at once and without effort. This is so true that some writers consider the precepts of the second class to be self-evident.

Proof 3. History and observation show that, at all times and in all regions of the world, men have possessed such knowledge.

92. **Objections.**

1. Some Indian tribes think a man has a right to kill his parents when they are old and infirm. Therefore the primary principles of the natural law are not known to all. *Answer.* These men certainly have given proof that they believed it wrong to slay the innocent. At the same time they considered that filial

piety enjoins relief to afflicted parents. This relief they judged they were giving by depriving their aged parents of life which had become a painful burden to the latter. To discern, in this confusion of obligation, the moral evil of their act of homicide, required a rather intricate process of reasoning, the conclusion of which belongs to the third class of precepts under the natural law. Our thesis, however, does not maintain that knowledge of this kind must be universal.

2. The Spartans of old approved in their children the vice of theft. *Answer.* Here, too, was a confusion of obligation. The Spartans held that the protection of the country was life's highest duty. Hence, though reprobating theft in general, they approved it in so far as the act was intended to develop military sagacity.

93. **Thesis XII.** *Human laws derive their binding force from the natural law, and ultimately from God.*

Explanation. We are not speaking here of every rule laid down by men, but of laws in the strict meaning of the term. Laws thus understood can be enacted by a perfect community only. As the State (the supreme society in the natural order), and the Church (which holds the same place in the supernatural order), are the only perfect societies, it follows that only the State and the Church can enact laws in the strict meaning of the term.

Proof 1. The chief dictate of the natural law is that we should observe right order in our free acts (No. 84). Now, right order requires that the members of a perfect community should obey all those rational directions which are given by him who has charge over the community—*i. e.*, that they should obey all laws. Therefore the natural law requires the observance of human laws. Moreover, the natural law derives its binding force from God; therefore the obligation to obey human laws, which flows directly from the natural law, proceeds ultimately from the same Divine source.

Proof 2. Once we grant that human laws can impose a moral obligation, it is easy to prove that their binding power is derived from God. For this power supposes superiority over the consciences of men. But whence do men derive such superiority? Not from themselves, because all men are equal by their nature. This power, therefore, must be derived from God, who alone is the superior of all men and has power over their consciences.

94. **Objections.**
   1. The laws of men are sometimes opposed to the laws of God; therefore human laws do not derive their binding force from God. *Answer.* Such enactments are not laws, and are falsely so called. A rule for human action which is opposed to God's law cannot be for the true good of the community.
   2. Sometimes the laws of the State are opposed to those of the Church. Therefore both cannot come from God. *Answer.* The laws of the State and those of the Church cannot clash if they are just. In case of dispute, the presumption for justness must be in favor of the higher community, the Church of God.

ARTICLE II. CONSCIENCE APPLYING THE MORAL LAW.

95. **Conscience** is the human intellect applying the general principles of morals to individual acts. The term, as employed in Moral Philosophy, means not an examination into one's past deeds, but a judgment on acts about to be performed. In judging whether an individual act is morally

good or evil, the intellect forms, explicitly or implicitly, a syllogism, the major of which is a known principle of morality, the minor a particular fact, and the conclusion a practical judgment, which is called a dictate of conscience. For instance,—a lie is never allowed; but to say that I have never sinned would be a lie; therefore, I am not allowed to say that I have never sinned. Conscience, then, may be defined as a practical judgment formed by reasoning from a universal principle to a particular fact, whereby I decide whether a certain individual act ought to be done or omitted, or whether it may be done or omitted, at my choice.

96. My conscience, with regard to any particular act may be *correct* or *erroneous*; its judgment may be *certain* or *doubtful*; the doubt may be concerning a *law* or a *fact*. A doubtful judgment is called an *opinion*; the reasons in favor of an opinion constitute its *probability*. In matters pertaining to conscience, we can seldom have the strictest certitude, such namely as excludes all possibility of error. However, moral certitude, which excludes a prudent doubt (Log. 79, etc.) is sufficient to safeguard moral rectitude. Hence, a **certain dictate of conscience** means a practical judgment free from a prudent doubt in regard to error. Moreover, it may happen that two honest men act in diametrically opposite ways about the same matter, and each may be morally certain that he is right. If I make a mistake through no fault of my own, my judgment is erroneous though it may be morally certain. In such a case I am said to be *invincibly ignorant* of the truth. If, however, the error is due to my own fault, my ignorance is *vincible*.

97. **Thesis XIII.** *Conscience when certain must be obeyed, whether it be correct or invincibly erroneous.*

Proof. We are bound to obey the law rationally—*i. e.*, as our intellect makes known to us the application of the law. But when conscience is certain, our intellect makes known to us the application of the law with certainty, whether our judgment in the matter be correct or invincibly erroneous. Therefore, conscience when certain must be obeyed, whether it be correct or invincibly erroneous.

98. Conscience is said to be doubtful, when the motive for believing that a particular law does not exist, or that it is not applicable to the case in hand is based on **an opinion more or less probable**—*i. e.*, more or less well founded.

1. An opinion is *slightly or barely probable* when it rests on very weak motives.
2. It is *probable*, or plausible, when supported by solid reasons, though stronger reasons may uphold the contradictory opinion.
3. It is *equally probable* with the contradictory opinion when both are supported by equally plausible reasons.
4. It is *more probable*, when the reasons favoring the opinion are stronger than those opposed to it.
5. It is *most probable*, when the arguments on which it rests are very strong, while those for the contradictory opinion are very weak.

99. Doubt, as affecting conscience is either **speculative** or **practical**. It is a **practical** doubt, if it regards the formal liceity of a particular act which is about to be performed. Hence, if I act with a practical doubt, I do not know whether or not I am doing wrong and displeasing God; for example: everything considered, I am in doubt whether I shall do wrong by reading a certain book which, I have reason to think, is dangerous to Faith.

Doubt is **speculative** when it concerns the premises of a syllogism, the conclusion of which is a dictate of conscience:

that is, if I doubt either that a certain law exists, or, granting its existence, that it is applicable to this particular case. I doubt, for example, whether by a law of the Church a certain Saturday of the year is a fast day, or, knowing that such a law exists, whether to-day is that particular Saturday; or, again, whether I am excused from fasting to-day by present illness.

100. **Thesis XIV.** *It is never right to act with a practical doubt of conscience.*

Proof. To act with a practical doubt of conscience is equivalent to saying: "I may break God's law, and so displease Him by doing this act, yet I will do it any way." But this is never right, because it is a manifest proof of an evil disposition to do the act, even if it were known to be prohibited, and hence shows contempt for God's law.

101. **What then must we do**, in order to avoid acting with a practical doubt of conscience? We may abstain from acting, if the matter so permits; or we may choose the safer side, that, namely, by which we fulfill the obligation in question; or we may remove the practical doubt. This removal we can sometimes effect by a more careful examination into the principles or facts involved, or by inquiring from competent authorities whether such a law exists, or whether it is applicable to this particular case. This would be to solve the speculative doubt, and is the direct method of getting rid of the practical doubt. But, if we are indeed so circumstanced that it is impossible to make use of the direct method, we may, nevertheless, get rid of the practical doubt, and act in the matter with safety, by applying to the difficulty the reflex principle of moral conduct: "A doubtful law has no binding force."

102. A course of conduct is called **safe**, if it excludes all danger of formal wrong. Yet one course may be **safer** than

another, for we can make assurance doubly sure by avoiding the possibility of even material wrong. The less safe course, however, must so guard me from formal wrong that I cannot be justly blamed for adopting it. Still, the fact that one opinion is safer than another, does not by itself make it the more probable of the two. Thus, if a neighbor has a less probable claim to a house in my possession, the safer course for me to follow, that I may avoid all possibility of doing him an injustice, would be to give up my claim in his favor; and yet, in point of genuineness, my neighbor's title is supposed to be less probable than mine.

103. **Thesis XV.** *When a certain end is absolutely to be secured, we must choose the safer way of securing it.*

Explanation. Since the end in this case is absolutely to be secured, I ought, if it were possible, to use means which are absolutely reliable or certain, for the means should be proportionate to the end. But it is here supposed that none of the means available is absolutely reliable, but that each is supported by probability only, one of the means having a higher degree of probability than any other. In this case, we maintain, with all moralists of standing, that the safer way, that, namely, which has the more probable opinion in its favor, must be followed in practice.

Proof. If I choose the less safe way, I freely make less certain the acquisition of an absolutely necessary end. But freely to lessen the certainty of attaining an absolutely necessary end is wrong. Therefore, I may not in this case choose the less safe way; on the contrary, I am bound to follow the safer way.

Thus, on the principle that Baptism is absolutely necessary for salvation, the Church baptizes converts, if their former baptism is doubtful. On this principle, too, physicians are not allowed, if sure remedies are at hand, to experiment with doubtful medicines upon their patients, whose health they are bound by their engagements to secure.

104. But when there is question of **the mere liceity of an act**, am I bound to adopt the more probable opinion? In other words, when, according to one probable opinion, the law requires a certain act of me, and, according to another probable opinion, such a requirement does not exist, am I bound to observe the law which probably has never been enacted? Or again, am I bound to observe an existing law in circumstances to which the law-giver probably never intended it to be applied?

On **various theories** various answers are given to this question:

> 1. *Rigorists* say: As long as any doubt remains that the law does not exist, the law must be obeyed, though, most probably, the law does not exist.
> 2. *Tutiorists* say: The law must be obeyed unless the opinion favoring an easier course be far more probable.
> 3. *Probabiliorists* say: Obey the law unless the opinion favoring an easier course be more probable.
> 4. *Probabilists* allow a free choice, provided the easier course has solid probability in its favor, even though the other course has greater probability.
> 5. *Laxists* permit liberty of choice even when the easier course is only slightly or barely probable. This last view, and that which requires for the liceity of an act certitude that it is not forbidden, have both been condemned by the Church.

105. **Thesis XVI.** *In questions of mere liceity, we may follow the easier course if there is a solidly probable opinion in its favor.*

Proof. A doubtful law has no binding force. But that law against whose existence a solidly probable opinion militates is a doubtful law. Therefore I am not bound to follow such a law. The principle, "A doubtful law has no binding force," which is received as an axiom, is apparent from the fact that such a law is wanting in an essential feature required for binding force, viz., full promulgation. If reasonable efforts have been made to remove the doubt, yet without success, we may conclude that the law, if it exists, has not been sufficiently promulgated.

106. **Objections:**

1. If the thesis is true, I am allowed to do wrong. *Answer.* We are never allowed to do formal wrong, *i. e.*, what we know to be wrong; but we are not always forbidden to do what is materially wrong, to do that, namely, which we do not know to be wrong.

2. But the law may be certain and only the application of it uncertain; I know, for instance, that I must abstain from meat on Friday, but I do not know whether this is Friday. *Answer.* The same rule holds for the application of the law as for its doubtful existence. If, after trying in vain to obtain enlightenment on the subject, I have a solidly probable opinion that to-day is not Friday, I may reason that the law of abstinence as affecting this particular case is a doubtful one, and therefore, for this particular application, has no binding force.

Article III. The Sanction of the Moral Law.

107. **The sanction of a law** is the provision of reward for the observance of the law and of punishment for its violation.

That sanction is called *perfect*, which is sufficient to make it a matter of every one's highest interest to observe the law. If the sanction falls short of this, it is said to be *imperfect*.

108. **Thesis XVII.** *The sanction appertaining to the natural law, though imperfect in this life, is perfect in the life to come.*

Part I. There is an imperfect sanction in this life. Proof. We know from the experience of mankind that the observance of the natural law usually brings with it certain forms of happiness, such as peace of mind, friendship, honor, a fair supply of earthly possessions, health and longevity; and that frequent violation of the law entails all of life's miseries, such as disquiet of mind, dishonor, poverty, disease, and often an early death. Hence it is evident that the natural law has some sanction in this life. Yet this sanction is very imperfect. Oftentimes the virtuous endure great misery in this life, while, on the other hand, evil doers are often comparatively prosperous and apparently triumphant in their wickedness. Moreover, the perfect sanction of the law requires that the rewards held out for its observance should exceed as recompense all inconvenience and suffering that may be incurred by observing the law, and that the penalties threatened should be greater than any emoluments or advantages that may be obtained by violating the law. Now, what reward, for example, can be given in this life to a man that dies for the truth? Is it the renown of a noble deed? But death makes the enjoyment of renown on earth an impossibility for him. Or again, does the weak remorse of the apostate match the advantage which his base denial of the Faith has gained in the preservation of his life? Therefore, the rewards and punishments of this life do not form a perfect sanction of the natural law.

Part II. A perfect sanction in the next life. Proof. Since

God wills the observance of the law which He has impressed upon the hearts of men, His wisdom requires Him to use the proper means to secure that observance. But the only means proper to secure this end without destroying human liberty is to propose adequate rewards and punishments, that is, to establish a perfect sanction of the law. Therefore a perfect sanction of the law exists. But since the sanction in this life is imperfect, it follows that there must be a perfect sanction in the next life.

109. We know that all men can attain the perfect happiness for which their nature longs insatiably. (Thesis IV.) It is clear, also, that this happiness, our *summum bonum*, or greatest good, the possession of God Himself (Thesis VI.), is **the chief sanction of the observance of the moral law:** it is the highest, the most complete, the most appropriate reward of the virtue practised in this life. Can any form of happiness be higher or more complete than the everlasting possession of God? The appropriateness of such a reward is apparent from the nature of virtue, which consists in the observance of the moral law, and is the direct means to the attainment of our last end. What then could be more appropriate than that virtue's reward should be the perfect possession of that towards which its endeavors tend?

110. Since vice consists essentially in a willful turning away from our last end, it becomes evident, by a process of reasoning similar to that followed above, that the privation of the possession of God is the natural and **chief punishment of the wicked.** Now, two ways are possible by which the wicked might be deprived of their last end, and so be disappointed of the only object that can satisfy the insatiable craving of their nature. One way is by the soul's utter annihilation after death; the other is by a future life of despair, in which the soul must

evermore be tormented by vain yearnings for the Good which it despised and rejected in the days of its trial on earth. We know from Revelation that the wicked who die impenitent shall be condemned to eternal sufferings. Natural reason, however, could not, of itself, give us certainty on this point. Yet it belongs to Moral Philosophy to show that this doctrine, far from being unreasonable, is in perfect accord with rational principles. Omitting the arguments adduced in our Psychology (Ment. Phil., No. 215), we shall merely disprove the possibility of the soul's annihilation, the only other way of depriving man of the last end which he has forfeited. If annihilation were possible, the perfect sanction of the natural law would be impossible. A sanction is not perfect that does not make it every man's highest interest to choose, in the face of the greatest temptation, the right rather than the wrong. Now, surely, annihilation would not be, on many occasions and for many persons, a perfect sanction. Are there not many persons in the world around us who would choose annihilation after death, rather than deny themselves unlawful gratifications? Besides, what retribution would then be in store for the crime of suicide?

111. Some have pleaded for the existence of another state of probation after death. But such a theory only shifts the difficulty without solving it. For, if at the end of the second probation some souls should persevere in their wickedness, shall there be a third trial,—and a fourth, and so on, forever? As the series of trials cannot go on without end, and as it is likely that some souls would persist in malice through multiplied probations, these souls must at last enter upon a fixed state of disappointment and despair. Hence, if this state must be entered upon finally, there is no reason why the first trial should not be decisive. In the second place, such an

arrangement would take from the punishment sanctioning the law its deterrent force. If, despite the present widespread belief of immediate retribution after death, so many are hopelessly wicked, how much more grievous and wicked would be the violations of the law if men were convinced that, in the next life, they should have an opportunity of averting the everlasting doom of sin!

112. Moreover, since the soul by its nature is immortal (Ment. Phil., No. 213 *et seq.*), it would be unreasonable to admit the possibility of the soul's annihilation.

Should it be objected against us, that eternal punishment is repugnant to the infinite mercy of God, we should answer that the justice of God is infinite as well as His mercy. Besides, eternal punishment is not only a vindication of right order, it is also deterrent and remedial. The consideration of that terrific retribution is calculated to keep to the narrow path of virtue many who are sorely tempted to stray therefrom, and to call back those who have left it for the perfidious ways of iniquity.

A suspicion may sometimes lurk in the mind that eternal punishment, though God has an absolute right to inflict it, is after all an excess of rigor and therefore unjust, because there would be no proportion between an eternity of suffering and the temporal duration of man's evil deeds. The difficulty arises from our failure to comprehend the malice of sin. The gravity of an offense is to be measured not by its duration only, but especially by the dignity of the person offended. Now the dignity of God is infinite; accordingly, an offense against His Sovereign Majesty is objectively infinite, and demands an infinite compensation. This a creature cannot give, because it is essentially finite; the nearest approach to an equivalent is an everlasting retribution.

BOOK II.

THE RIGHTS AND DUTIES OF INDIVIDUALS.

113. Thus far we have considered human acts in their relation to our final beatitude, and the natural law as directing these acts to their appointed end. We shall next proceed to apply this law to man's rights and duties. In the present book we shall treat of the rights and duties of **man viewed as an individual.** In the last book we shall treat of his social rights and duties.

CHAPTER I.

RIGHTS AND DUTIES IN GENERAL.

114. To say that a man has a **right** to a thing, means that he has a certain power over it. Evidently, however, physical power does not of itself constitute a right. The highwayman's power over the traveler's money gives him no right thereto. A right, then, belongs to the moral order. It is an *inviolable moral power* belonging to one man, which, therefore, *all other men are bound to respect*.

115. In every right four things are to be taken into account: (a) the *subject*, *i. e.*, the person possessing the right; (b) the *term*, including all those who are bound to respect the right; (c) the *title*, or reason on which the right is founded; (d) the *matter*, or that to which the subject has a right. The matter may be my own act or the act of another person; that is, I may have the right to perform a certain act or to require the performance or the omission of an act on the part of another. Thus in N.'s right to the house which he owns, N. himself is the subject, all other persons constitute the term, his payment of the purchase money agreed upon is the title, and the ownership of the house is the matter. He has a right to occupy the house, to prevent others from dwelling in it, or to require the party who leases it to pay the stipulated rent.

116. A right possessed by one person involves, on the part of another or of others, the obligation to respect that right. This obligation is called a *duty*. We may therefore define **duty** in the abstract as a moral bond or obligation of doing

or omitting certain acts in favor of another person. The act itself that ought to be done or omitted is the concrete duty. Every duty then supposes a corresponding right, and every right a duty: **right and duty are correlative and inseparable.** Hence brute animals can have no rights, for they have no duties or moral obligations, since by their irrational nature they are incapable of voluntary acts. We are under obligation to abstain from cruelty to animals, not because they have rights, but because such conduct is unworthy of our rational nature. Insane persons and infants have rights radically, which all are bound to respect; yet by reason of their mental helplessness they are exempt from performing duties.

117. Every duty or obligation supposes that some one who has power to bind the consciences of men has imposed the obligation. Now, moral acts, we know from the preceding book, are such as are in conformity with the moral law, which has God for its author. As every moral obligation is necessarily associated with a moral act, it depends, immediately or remotely, for its binding force upon the moral law and the Divine Author of the law. Therefore, the true rights and duties of man come from God; and they cannot be correctly understood if considered apart from their dependence upon God.

118. Rights and duties are inseparable; yet it may be asked, **which is prior?** Do the duties which rest upon us precede in the order of nature and of supposition the corresponding rights, or is the converse true?

>1. *Absolutely*, or in the formal concept of right and duty, right is prior to duty. Right is a moral power existing in one person, which gives rise to an obligation in another. Consequently, the right is the cause

of the obligation, and every cause is prior, in the order of nature and of supposition, to its effect.

2. Since *God cannot be bound* or limited, He has no duties towards His creatures, although He possesses sovereign rights over all creation.

3. Hence, *man has no rights with regard to God;* he has duties only. These duties, which God has imposed, confer upon him a right to the means required to attain the end of his existence. Thus man's dependence upon God is a duty prior to all his rights, and, at the same time, it is the source of all his rights. Once God has deigned to bestow upon us the right of existence, He owes it to His own infinite attributes to perfect His gift by endowing us with all the rights necessary for our existence as men.

4. A man's God-given rights impose obligations or duties on other men to respect his rights. Hence, *in the relations of men with one another*, right is prior to duty.

119. **Rights are variously divided** into *connatural* and *acquired, alienable* and *inalienable, perfect* and *imperfect.*

1. *Connatural* rights are those which are inseparable from the nature of man as a person. Such are the rights to life and limb, to personal integrity, to liberty of action within just limits, to specific equality as a member of the human family. *Acquired* rights come to a man in virtue of his own exertions, or of acts done by others in his favor; for example, rights to property, to franchise, to office, are acquired rights.

2. *Inalienable* rights are those which a man cannot renounce or transfer to another, because they are necessary to the attainment of his last end. All other rights

are called alienable. "We hold these truths to be self-evident," says our Declaration of Independence, "that all men are created equal; that they are endowed by their Creator with certain inalienable rights; that among them are life, liberty, and the pursuit of happiness."

3. *Perfect* or strict rights are of such a kind that the corresponding duties are matters of commutative justice. *Imperfect* rights are not so definite; they are founded not on justice but on claims of gratitude or of honor, or on some similar title.

120. **Rights in conflict.** Rights cannot strictly be said to conflict. We may meet with conflicting claims to the same thing, or apparent rights in conflict, but of these only one can be a real right. For, by the nature of a right, its existence in one person imposes an obligation upon all others to respect that right. Consequently, conflicting rights is a contradiction in terms, because "I am bound to respect something" and "I am not so bound" are evidently contradictory propositions. When two claims conflict, the right disputed must be decided to belong to the claimant that has the true title, or at least the better title. Such a decision is not always easy, especially as men are naturally prepossessed in favor of their own interests, and on this account they are often forced to make use of arbitration and law courts.

121. The following **principles regarding conflicting claims** are obvious: of two claims otherwise equal that should prevail—

1. Which is more necessary for the attainment of man's last end: thus, the right to life takes precedence of that to property. Hence, if a man who is suffering extreme poverty has instant need of food, he possesses

the right to supply his need from the provisions of others who are not in equal or greater need.

2. Which concerns the good of the greater number. For this reason, the common good takes precedence of private good, as when a citizen has to expose his life in defense of the State.

3. Which is more probably genuine: thus, a man possessing an object which he acquired in good faith can continue to hold it till a better claim be proved.

122. **Various classes of duties** correspond to the various classes of rights: to the natural rights of one person correspond the *natural* duties of others; to acquired rights, *adventitious* duties; to imperfect rights, *imperfect* duties. *Positive* duties which are based on positive or affirmative precepts of the law, oblige us to perform certain acts; while *negative* duties, which are based on negative precepts, oblige us to abstain from certain acts. Positive duties do not require us to act at every moment, but only at certain times; negative duties, however, oblige us to abstain at all times from the forbidden acts.

We have duties to *God*, to *ourselves*, and to *our neighbor*. These three classes of duties we shall examine severally in the three following chapters.

CHAPTER II.

OUR DUTIES TO GOD.

123. **Our duties to God take precedence of all other duties:** (a) *Logically*, because God is the First Cause, upon whom we, as contingent beings and effects of His creative power, depend for the beginning and continuance of our existence. Upon this dependence are founded all our rights and duties. (b) *Morally*, because God is our last end; and all morality consists in directing our acts to our last end.

124. **Religion,** *objectively* considered, is the sum total of all our duties to God. It is not a thing of human invention, but, as Cicero observes: "It is to be found in every land; for nature knows how to worship God, and no man is ignorant of the law by which it is enjoined."

Considered *subjectively*, religion is the moral virtue by which man renders due homage to God as the first beginning and last end of all things. Hence, to acknowledge our entire dependence on Him is the primary act of this virtue. We acknowledge the dependence of our entire existence by *adoration*, of our intellect by *faith*, of our will by *love*. These, accordingly, are the three fundamental duties of religion. Though God has no need of these acts for Himself, still He is the author of the moral order by which these acts are enjoined, and He owes it to His own sanctity to exact the observance of the moral order.

Article I. Adoration.

125. Thesis I. *All men are bound to render to God the worship of interior and exterior adoration.*

Proof. Reason dictates that a subject or dependent show honor to his ruler, and that such honor be proportioned to the ruler's dignity and the subject's dependence. But all men depend in every respect upon God, their Creator and Sovereign Lord, the Ruler of the Universe, the Master of life and death. Moreover, God is worthy of infinite honor. Therefore man owes God the greatest possible honor, such honor as is incommunicable to any created being.

The honor rendered in acknowledgement of God's sovereign dominion is called *adoration*. This, we maintain, ought to be both *interior* and *exterior*.

1. *Interior adoration.* We owe God the reverence and honor of our highest faculties, *i. e.*, of our intellect and will. But operations of these faculties are interior; they are not, in themselves, perceptible by the senses. Therefore, we owe God the worship of interior adoration.

2. *Exterior adoration.* Man owes God the homage not of a part of his being, but of his whole being. His body, as well as his soul, is entirely dependent upon God, and should, therefore, contribute by outward or bodily action to the extrinsic glory of God. (No. 22.) Besides, on account of the close union between soul and body, interior reverence naturally finds expression in external action; and outward acts, in their turn, promote interior reverence. As outward action falls under the senses, our external reverence

helps our fellow-men to elicit and express the reverence and honor which they, too, owe to God.

126. Men are not isolated individuals, but they are, as we shall prove later on, naturally social beings. Hence, in this connection, we may insert a thesis on the worship which men in their social capacity owe to God.

Thesis II. *Men are obliged to render public worship to God.*

Proof 1. Society is natural to mankind; hence it comes from the Author of nature. Society, therefore, no less than private individuals, is dependent upon God, and owes Him the worship due to His infinite Majesty. Consequently, men are obliged, as members of society, to render to God the homage proper to society, which is the worship of public adoration.

Proof 2. The public acknowledgment of God's supreme dominion over all created things is necessary for the welfare of civil society; so much so, that a notorious infidel has said: "If a God did not exist, we should have to invent one for the public good." On this public acknowledgment are based, in great measure, the sanctity of oaths, the binding power of contracts, the strength of the marriage bond, the fidelity of subjects as well as the integrity of rulers, and consequently the stability of governments and civil constitutions. Hence, those who attack the worship of God are dangerous enemies of mankind, for they are endeavoring to sap the foundations of society.

127. **The vices directly opposed to religion** are impiety, idolatry, and superstition. *Impiety* is the refusal to give supreme honor to God. If it takes the positive form of direct dishonor to God, it is called *blasphemy*. *Idolatry* consists in worshiping a creature with an adoration due to God alone.

By *superstition* we mean certain practices, with a religious intent, that are irrational or unworthy of their purpose.

128. **The principal acts of adoration** are *prayer* and *sacrifice*, which have been practised by all nations from their beginning. The special forms that both should assume have not been determined by nature. Of course, God had the right to determine such forms by a supernatural Revelation and to make them obligatory upon all His subjects. No act of ours is sufficient by itself to regain the favor of our Creator if we have once lost it by sin; we could never know, except from a supernatural source, how to obtain the Divine pardon.

ARTICLE II. FAITH IN GOD'S WORD.

129. **Thesis III.** *All men are obliged to accept Divine Revelation, when it has been made known to them, and to believe the mysteries which it may contain.*

Explanation. We know indeed that a supernatural Revelation has been given to mankind. This, however, it is the province, not of Philosophy, but of Theology and kindred sciences to prove and discuss. Prescinding, therefore, from the actual state of things, we examine, from the standpoint of natural reason, what man's duties are in regard to Revelation if the latter should be made.

Part 1. Man is obliged to accept Divine Revelation. Proof. God is the Supreme Lord and Master of all His creatures. He has the right, therefore, to enjoin upon us the acceptance of certain truths which natural reason by itself is incapable of discovering, and to command the performance of certain acts of worship. This right connotes, on our part, the duty of accepting such truths and of performing such acts, when God's will in these matters shall have been made known to us.

Now this is to accept Divine Revelation. Consequently, we are obliged to accept Divine Revelation when it has been made known to us.

Part 2. Man is obliged to believe in revealed mysteries. *Proof.* A mystery is a truth which human reason cannot comprehend. We may understand the meaning of the subject and the predicate of the proposition in which the incomprehensible truth is enunciated; we may know that such a predicate belongs to such a subject, but we cannot perceive how or why they are thus connected. Even in the natural order, many of the physical phenomena are incomprehensible truths, and may, therefore, be called, in a certain sense, natural mysteries. Revealed or supernatural mysteries are those truths which can be learned only by Divine Revelation; for example, that the three Divine Persons are one God. Now, God's infinite knowledge necessarily includes truths which surpass our finite understanding; such truths He is surely able to make known to us, and He has the right to demand our belief in the same as an homage of our understanding. Therefore, we are under obligation to believe the mysteries which God may be pleased to reveal.

130. **Objections.**
    1. It is unworthy of a man to believe what he does not understand. *Answer.* If such belief were without a sufficient reason, yes; but if it is supported by the best of reasons, namely, the infallible authority of God, belief is truly worthy of man, and the contrary course would be most unreasonable.

    2. Dogmatic teaching enslaves the intellect. *Answer.* An entire reliance upon authority in every science would be detrimental to intellectual development. But to reject the momentous truths of Revelation, because

they come from authority, would be more unreasonable than to refuse belief in the existence of the Roman Empire, because we must depend ultimately for our knowledge of this historic fact upon human testimony.

3. The knowledge of mysteries is useless. *Answer.* On the contrary, it is most useful; besides giving us an occasion to honor God by the homage of our intellect, it wonderfully and consolingly expands our knowledge of God and of our own destinies.

4. Dogmatic teaching begets intolerance. *Answer.* Truth begets a *theoretic* intolerance, or a firmness of conviction which is intolerant of error. But we deny that such a state of mind, whether it rests upon authoritative teaching, or upon demonstration, causes *practical* intolerance, or an unjust interference with civil and religious liberty. The persecution of the Church in recent times, carried on in many lands by the opponents of Revelation, shows what begets intolerance.

131. If God deigns to bestow a Revelation upon us, He must necessarily give us the means of recognizing it as such. Chief among these means are *miracles* and *prophecies*. **Miracles** are effects perceptible by the senses, which transcend the powers and the order of all nature. We have demonstrated (Ment. Phil., Cosmol., Chap. III.) that miracles are possible, and can be known as such with certainty. **Prophecies** are accurate predictions of such future events as depend upon free causes, and cannot be known in advance with certainty, except by the omniscient God.

132. **Thesis IV.** *Miracles and prophecies are infallible proofs of a Divine Revelation.*

Explanation. In this thesis we maintain that if, unmistakably, miracles have been worked or prophecies been made in confirmation of a doctrine, that doctrine is thereby known to be approved by the Creator as His own Divine Revelation. The immediate inference from the thesis would be that such a doctrine must be accepted by all men.

Proof. A true miracle can be wrought by God alone. Hence, it is a Divine seal, stamped as it were upon the doctrine, in express confirmation of which the miracle is worked. The Divine origin of such a doctrine, therefore, is infallibly true, because it is impossible for God to affix His seal to a falsehood.

A prophecy is an accurate prediction of a future event that is not dependent upon necessary causes. But God alone is the author of such a prediction, for He alone can possess such knowledge. Therefore, prophecies made in confirmation of a doctrine which is published as coming from God, are infallible proofs that such a doctrine is a Divine Revelation.

133. God is at perfect liberty to choose the **manner of His Revelation.** As a matter of fact, however, He has chosen to manifest it to the vast majority of men, not *immediately*, *i. e.*, by directly acting upon the intellect with an overpowering illumination, but *mediately, i. e.*, through the medium of other men whom He has commissioned to publish His revealed truths. Thus, the evidence of Revelation does not overmaster the rational faculties, but leaves a man free to accept it, and, in this manner, to increase his merit. This acceptance is an act of the highest prudence, while the rejection of Divine Revelation would be unreasonable and a grievous wrong. Indeed, from man's complete dependence upon God, and his consequent duty to reverence the Divine teach-

ings and to accept them with loving promptness, it follows, logically, that every one who conceives a well-grounded suspicion that a Divine Revelation has been made, is obliged in conscience to inquire into the matter with more than ordinary diligence.

134. Thesis V. *Indifference in the matter of religion is a grievous wrong.*

Proof. This indifference may be theoretical or practical. *Theoretical* indifference is an opinion that all systems or forms of religion, though contradictory to one another, are equally pleasing to God and useful to man. This doctrine is false, and an insult to God. It is false, because all truth, and, *a fortiori*, revealed truth, is one and not self-contradictory. It is an insult to God, because it represents Infinite Truth as pleased with error. *Practical* indifference is a refusal to give God the homage which man owes Him essentially (Thesis I.). As both kinds of indifference imply a great moral disorder, they are both grievously wrong.

135. It is evident:

1. That God cannot make contradictory revelations. Therefore, there can be **only one true religion** in the world; for all systems of religion contradict one another on some points of doctrine.

2. That God cannot be glorified or pleased by falsehood. In this, as in other matters, He overlooks mistakes that are caused by invincible ignorance. Nevertheless, once a reasonable suspicion concerning this matter exists in the mind, a man is obliged to do his utmost in order to discover the truth about supernatural Revelation, namely, whether a Revelation has been made and where it may be found.

3. That, if God has made a Revelation to direct men to

their last end, He must, in His infinite wisdom, have provided reliable means to distinguish it from all false systems usurping its place.

136. Objections.
1. One does enough, if he is an honest man. *Answer.* A man who does not practise religion is not an honest man, for he defrauds God of the worship which is justly His due.
2. Among so many jarring creeds, it is impossible to discover the true religion. *Answer.* Still, one form of religion is divinely true, which alone can be pleasing to God. Now, God's providence and goodness are doubted by thinking that the true form of religion is beyond the reach of an earnest mind seeking the truth and at the same time humbly asking God's aid to find it.
3. No one should change his religion. *Answer.* Certainly not, unless his religion is false.
4. Then every man on earth ought to set about inquiring into the truth of his religion. *Answer.* Only those need inquire who have good reason for doubting the truth of their religion.

137. History attests and Theology confirms the facts, that a Revelation was made to mankind in the very beginning; that this was subsequently amplified and developed by further revelations; that it was finally perfected by the teachings of the Son of God Himself, and that this **Christian Revelation** has been entrusted, in its completeness, to an infallible Church, to be preserved and expounded until the end of time. These are truths beyond the reach of Philosophy. Nevertheless, Reason leads us by the radiance of her own natural light to the portal of supernatural religion, and is

there met by a Heavenly guide, with a brightness of illumination so dazzling that all natural lights in its presence must pale to dimness. In that sacred temple, across whose threshold she may pass with man, Reason finds many truths above her grasp, which she calls mysteries, yet none are opposed to her own inherent principles. There she may abide in peace under the guidance of the Divine Spirit, who rules there.

138. **Was a Divine Revelation necessary for mankind?** That form of Revelation which declares the Beatific Vision to be man's supernatural destiny and teaches him the supernatural means to secure it was not necessary for the attainment of a merely natural end. Absolutely or intrinsically considered, the latter could be attained by reason unassisted supernaturally: it would be physically possible; but, for the overwhelming majority, such an event would be morally impossible. This, too, is the lesson taught by History on its every page. The nations of the earth, even the most highly civilized, had fallen, despite the teachings of primeval Revelation, into the grossest idolatry. Besides, how strangely and wildly some of the most rarely gifted minds have erred in matters of the greatest importance! In our own times also we are made painfully aware of the deplorable tendency of self-sufficient souls to mistake the truth respecting man's duties to God. False philosophies,—Pantheism, Positivism, Agnosticism, Materialism,—are, alas! too widespread and too notoriously prominent in the world of thought to leave us ground for thinking that mankind could have reached even a natural end without the assistance of a supernatural Revelation.

139. Although there should exist many philosophical teachers holding perfectly correct doctrines on the duties of man, still, countless multitudes could not, by this natural means alone, become truly enlightened. Such enlightenment can be

accomplished in **only two ways**, by reasoning and by proclaiming truths with infallible authority. In neither way, however, could the desired effect be brought about for the masses. It could not be done by *reasoning*, since few, comparatively, would be able to follow the required processes of thought. Nor could *authority* be of avail, in the hypothesis of a purely natural order. Other men, holding false doctrines, might claim equal authority, and then how could the dispute be settled by natural means to the satisfaction of the people? What natural sign would mark the authoritative teachers of mankind and distinguish them from the propagators of error?

ARTICLE III. THE LOVE OF GOD.

140. **Love** is an act of the will by which we tend to good. We render to God the due homage of our will by loving Him above all things, just as by valuing His word above all other testimony we offer Him the homage of our understanding. Our love is well ordered when it tends towards an object according to the measure of true good which the intellect perceives in that object. Now, God is the highest good, not merely relatively, but absolutely the highest good, for He is the Infinite Good. Therefore, if we love God according to the measure of His goodness, we must love Him as the Supreme Good, and for His own sake, because He deserves infinite love. This perfect love for God is the love of **benevolence** or **friendship**; a friend being one to whom we wish well, not for our own satisfaction only, but for his sake.

141. Yet we also understand that God is the source of immeasurable good for us. This happens in many ways, but chiefly because our ultimate happiness consists in possessing Him for eternity. To love God for our own **sakes** is a

love of desire or hope. It is well ordered, however, since it fulfills the requirements stated above. Our intellect, indeed, perceives that God is not only the highest good in Himself, but also the good most conducive to our own happiness. Still, this love is imperfect; for, in tending towards God, it does not regard the highest good, namely, God's supreme excellence. Moreover, to be acceptable to God, our love for Him, whether perfect or imperfect, must always be a love of *preference*, that is, a love which prefers God to all things else. We need not, however, constantly perform acts of love for God, this duty being founded upon the positive precepts, which oblige us to act only at certain times.

CHAPTER III.

OUR DUTIES TO OURSELVES.

142. Strictly speaking, we do not owe **duties to ourselves**, since a duty is a moral bond obliging us to respect the rights of others. In many cases I can remit the debt due me from my neighbor and thus dispense him from certain duties towards myself, but I cannot free myself from one of those duties which I am said to owe to myself. Such duties, however, we do not really owe to ourselves but to God, for we belong to him absolutely and entirely; hence, we are His property and His servants. To Him we owe the duty of taking care of ourselves and of reasonably promoting our own good. Such, in Moral Philosophy, is the meaning of the expression *our duties to ourselves.*

143. **What duties then do we owe to ourselves?** Evidently in this matter we are obliged to observe the most general principle of the moral law, "do that which good order requires." Now, the first requirement of good order is that we tend toward the end for which we have been made. In brief, therefore, my duties to myself consist in directing my voluntary acts in such a manner as to attain my last end. In detail:

   1. My last end and the way to reach it are made known to me through my *intellect;* hence I have a duty to develop my intellect in order to perceive, with increasing clearness, the best means for attaining my

end, and, consequently, for understanding the law of God and its application to myself.

2. The moral order regards free acts, or acts of the *will;* hence, I ought to strengthen the will by training it to follow the guidance of reason.

3. But this implies that I must control my *passions*, which tend to hinder my will from obeying such guidance.

4. To accomplish all this and to fill the place allotted to me by Providence, I am bound in duty to take reasonable care of my *life and the health of my body;* besides, I must endeavor to acquire such *temporal goods* as may help me to lead a moral life.

5. For like reasons, I must, to some extent, protect my *honor* or reputation.

144. **Thesis VI.** *Suicide is never allowed.*

Proof. Suicide is the taking away of one's own life. But this is a usurpation of God's supreme dominion over life and death, and hence a grievous violation of the moral order. God has an absolute right to every moment of my existence and to all the honor I can give Him by fulfilling His sovereign will, even by patiently enduring the ills which He permits to befall me. Since, therefore, suicide is a great moral disorder, it can never be allowed.

Objections.

1. Courage is praiseworthy; it is exhibited in suicide. *Answer.* The man who commits suicide, is rash, not courageous, in attempting what he has no right to do, and, as Plato says in his dialogue called Phædo, he is a moral coward in running away from his post.

2. Of two evils we ought to choose the less grievous; but suicide is an evil less grievous than a life of sin.

Answer. There is here no matter for choice; we are not forced to sin; an act is not sinful, unless it is free. Besides, we are never permitted to do evil that good may result therefrom.

3. We must be willing to sacrifice our lives in order to possess God the sooner. *Answer.* We must be willing to die when God wills it and in the manner that pleases Him, but not in a way that would be a violation of His divine right. Such a violation would deprive us forever of the possession of God.

4. A criminal might be condemned to kill himself, as was the case with Socrates. *Answer.* No authority can oblige a person to do what is, in itself, morally evil.

145. Yet we may at times **expose our lives** to imminent danger, provided, as in the case of evil indirectly willed (No. 51), we do not directly intend our death, and the good to be thereby obtained is worthy of so great a risk. No one has a right to expose life or limb or health for a trifle, such as vain glory or the gratification of mere curiosity. But a sufficient reason might be found in the needs of our religion or of our country, the advancement of science, the relief of persons in distress, or in any other truly noble cause, when important results are to be attained which cannot be secured without such a risk.

CHAPTER IV.

OUR RIGHTS AND DUTIES TOWARDS OUR FELLOW-MEN.

146. Man has duties towards God and towards himself; in regard to his fellow-men he has both duties and rights. We are still speaking of man as an individual and not as a member of society. According to this view we shall next consider his duties to other men and his right to possess property.

ARTICLE I. THE LOVE WE OWE OUR FELLOW-MEN.

147. **Thesis VII.** *We must love our fellow-men as we love ourselves.*

Explanation. We do not say *as much* or as intensely as we love ourselves, for this would be impossible, but "as ourselves," that is, in a similar manner, by wishing them good things of the kind we desire for ourselves.

Proof. Right order, which is the foundation of all morality, requires the creature to conform his will to the will of the Creator. Now, the Creator wills the good of all men, namely, that they shall, of their own free will, attain their last end, and that they shall have all the necessary means to do so. This same, therefore, we must desire for our fellow-men; and this is to love our fellow-men as we love ourselves.

Right order requires also that every one shall make it his first duty to work out his own salvation; he is immediately and directly responsible for this. Hence, he must seek primarily to procure with most special care all things tending to this object, which is his own greatest good. Consequently every man must love himself more than he loves other men.

My love for other men is based on the fact of our common nature. All other men have the same specific nature as myself, but not the same identity or individuality; therefore, my love for all other men must be the same specifically, or of the same kind, as my love for myself; but it need not, in truth it cannot, be so intense, because I cannot be so completely identified with another person as with my individual self.

148. But according to the foregoing principle, does not **heroism,** by which men sacrifice themselves for the good of others, violate the rule of well-ordered love? Even here the principle holds true; for, though the hero may risk or sacrifice his life to save another person, yet he thereby endeavors to gain for himself a higher good than life. His heroic act of charity merits a greater reward in the next world than a prolonged life of ordinary virtue. Hence, he really seeks his own greater good, preferring a spiritual good to one that is temporal.

149. From the argument of the preceding thesis, it is apparent that, even in the natural order, our love for our fellow-men is based for its motive upon our love for God. Hence, we perceive that all our rights and duties are referred directly or indirectly to our dependence upon God.

The dictates of this general love may be thus expressed: "Never do to others what you would not wish them to do to you," and "do unto others as you would have others do unto you." The negative dictate of this law obliges always; the positive dictate obliges us to act on special occasions only, when others are in uncommon need of assistance. Our duty to render such assistance becomes urgent when they are in extreme necessity.

150. We are obliged to love all men; therefore, **we must love our enemies.** True, we may take whatever precautions sound reason approves, in order to protect our right against those who seek to injure us, but our object in so doing must be justice or the expediency of public or private good, and not personal revenge. It is not lawful to hate our enemies, for hatred is never a means to redress the wrong we may have suffered; nor are we allowed to injure them, unless the injury be done in self-defense (No. 164), and without violating the order of civil society. Nay even, we cannot rightfully exclude enemies from that general internal love which we owe to all men. They may, it is true, have done nothing to deserve such favor; yet, in common with ourselves, they are members of the human family, and made in a special manner to the image and likeness of God.

151. **Whom are we to love most?** Evidently, we ought to love those most who are most closely united to us by ties of nature, religion or civil society. Community of nature being the bond of love between man and his fellows, the more two parties have naturally in common, or the nearer they approach to identity by relationship of any kind, the greater ought to be their love for each other. Special effects of this love ought to be determined by the particular kind of relationship: to blood relations, we owe, especially, natural goods; to our brethren in the household of the Faith, spiritual goods; to our fellow-citizens, civil protection.

ARTICLE II. OUR DUTIES REGARDING THE MINDS AND WILLS OF OTHERS.

152. Duties to others founded on the mutual relationship of our minds are violated by all falsehood and, particularly,

by the propagation of false principles. Duties arising from the relationship of our wills are violated by bad example or scandal, which tends to deprave the wills of others.

153. A falsehood, or lie, is speech contrary to one's mind. By a falsehood, a contradiction is willfully established between a person's thoughts and the received expression of those thoughts. For this reason, a falsehood contains a moral disorder and is essentially wrong.

Lying must be distinguished from *equivocation* and *mental reservation*.

154. **Equivocation** consists in using an expression readily susceptible of two meanings, one false, the other true, which the listener or reader can, and often will, understand wrongly. Thus we read (Gen. xii. 13), that, on entering Egypt, Abraham instructed Sarai to call herself his sister, the Hebrew word for sister being often used to denote a near female relative. He did this because his life would not have been safe if she were known to be his wife. In the matter of liceity, equivocation is generally classed with mental reservation which is not purely mental.

155. "**Mental reservation** is the unexpressed qualification of a statement affecting or entirely altering its meaning as understood by the person addressed, generally so that the uttered statement is untrue, though with the qualification it is true." (Standard Dictionary, 1894.)

It consists, therefore, in withholding a circumstance by which a statement is qualified in such a manner that the statement is false as it stands, although it is true if joined to the qualifying circumstance. When it is *strictly mental, i. e.*, when there is nothing either in the words or in the circumstances that can prevent the hearer from being deceived, it is equivalent to a lie and therefore essentially wrong. But when the reservation is *not strictly mental*, it may be allowed at times; yet not without weighty reasons, else speech would become unreliable and social confidence would be impaired. If, however, reservation were never lawful, the common good or great private good would often have to be sacrificed without sufficient reason, for it may often happen that important secrets cannot be protected without mental reservation. One example will suffice: a man to whom an official secret has been intrusted may answer, if interrogated on the subject, that he does not know, meaning thereby that he does not know the matter in such a way as to be able to communicate it.

The objection may be raised that mental reservation is always wrong because it leads others into error, and, consequently, inflicts an injury upon them. We answer that he who uses a mental reservation, as an unavoidable means, intends directly to save a private person or the public from injury; and that, in so doing, he is not the cause but the justifiable occasion of error in the mind of the rash questioner.

156. **Thesis VIII.** *A lie is intrinsically evil.*

Proof 1. It is intrinsically evil to use a thing contrary to its natural end. But the natural end of speech is to communicate our thoughts to our fellow-men, and a lie is the contrary of the thoughts of him who utters it. Therefore, a lie is contrary to the natural end of speech and is intrinsically evil.

Proof 2. The universal shame attached to lying is an evident sign that, by the common consent of mankind, it is held to be wrong in itself. This is made clearer by the application of the simple text, "Do not do unto others, etc." Does any person wish to be deceived? Lying, then, is an evil to the intellect which no one wishes to suffer, for no one wishes to be deceived.

Proof 3. Man is by nature a social being; hence it is the will of the Author of Nature that he shall live in society. Therefore, whatever tends to subvert human society is intrinsically wrong. But lying tends to do this, because it weakens mutual confidence, which is essential for human society.

157. **Objections.**
 1. That cannot be wrong which all civilized nations allow in their courts of justice; but they allow the guilty to plead "not guilty." *Answer.* "Not guilty," pleaded in a criminal court, is an accepted technicality meaning "not proved guilty."
 2. That is not wrong which is related by Holy Scripture concerning virtuous men; but it is there related that Jacob said, "I am Esau, thy first-born (Gen. xxvii. 19). *Answer.* Jacob regarded himself, after purchasing Esau's right of primogeniture, as legally Esau the first-born. Besides, Holy Scripture does not approve all the deeds which it chronicles of good men.
 3. Our Blessed Saviour Himself declared that He was not going up to Jerusalem, and yet eventually He went thither (John vii. 8). *Answer.* Our Lord did not go up to Jerusalem on that particular festival day of which He was speaking at the time, but He went up on the third or fourth day afterwards.
 4. But He denied that He knew when the end of the world should come (Mark xiii. 32). *Answer.* Our Lord spoke mystically as man and not as God; so He was understood by His disciples, as in other like passages, *e. g.*, "My doctrine is not mine, but His that sent me."

158. **Thesis IX.** *We are obliged to refrain from giving scandal.*

Explanation. Our duty towards the will of our fellow-man amounts to this: that, in charity, we ought to aid him in the attainment of his highest good, and, in justice as well as in charity, we must never deter him therefrom. We may so deter him, and thus become accessory to another's wrongdoing, in various ways, and especially by bad example, all of which we include under the general term, scandal. For scandal may be given by any word or deed not entirely right, which is an occasion of wrongdoing on the part of others.

Proof. We are obliged to will that others should attain their last end (Thesis VII.). But to give scandal is to will the contrary, because it tends to lead men away from their last end. Therefore, we are obliged to refrain from giving scandal.

ARTICLE III. DUTIES REGARDING THE LIVES OF OTHERS.

159. Taking away another man's life is **homicide**. This, we shall see further on, may in special cases be justifiable, namely, in a just war (No. 263), in the infliction of the death penalty by the civil authority (No. 249), and in self-defense (No. 164). When homicide is not justifiable yet has extenuating circumstances, it is known as **manslaughter**; when committed with malice and full deliberation, it is called **murder**. In the law, murder is defined as "the killing of a man with malice prepense or aforethought."

160. The material world has been created for mankind; not for this or that individual man, not for any special class of men, but for every man and for all men. Each and every man is created for God and for his own final happiness, which is to be found in the everlasting possession of God. Considered in this light, *i. e.*, according to their nature, all men

are equal and independent of one another. It is not with man as with the brute creation. All other things have been made for him; he can, therefore, dispose of them for his own advantage, and he has the right of life and death over irrational animals. But man has been made for God alone; consequently, **to God alone belongs the right of life and death** over man. Besides, since man is bound to tend towards his last end, he has a natural right to the means necessary for this purpose. Now, life is such a means; it is the foundation or the indispensable condition of all other means. Therefore, every man has a right to life, which all other men are bound to respect.

161. **Thesis X.** *Murder is a great wrong.*

Proof. The violation of most important rights is a great wrong. But murder is such a violation: it is therefore a great wrong. Murder is a violation: 1. Of God's right over human life. 2. Of the murdered man's right to his own life, the foundation of his other rights and duties, and the means necessary to attain or increase his final beatitude. 3. Of the rights of society to one of its members, and to public peace and order. 4. Of the rights that bereaved relatives and friends have to the love and society of the murdered man. Though some of the latter evils may not exist in special cases, nevertheless the chief disorders are present in every murder.

162. **Objections.**

> 1. An act is good when its object, end, and circumstances are good; but such would be the case in, say, the murder of a persecutor of the Church. *Answer.* The object of the act, or the thing done (No. 47) is wrong, for it is a usurpation of God's absolute right over the life and death of man.
>
> 2. How then can it be right to kill a man in war?

Answer. The thesis treats of murder, but not of justifiable homicide. We shall see (No. 263) that God confers upon the State the right of waging a just war.

3. David killed the young man who had slain Saul. *Answer.* David acted in this case as a sovereign punishing crime.

4. Moses by his private authority slew an Egyptian. *Answer.* Moses was the divinely appointed deliverer of the chosen people. God, the master of life and death, inspired him to begin his task in this manner.

5. Inspiration cannot be claimed for Mathathias, who put an apostate to death by his own authority (Mach. ii. 24). *Answer.* Mathathias was high-priest and judge, and, as such, the executive of the Jewish law, which ordained death without trial to the introducer of idolatry.

163. **Thesis XI.** *Under certain conditions it is lawful, in self-defense, to kill an unjust aggressor.*

Explanation. The conditions are: 1. Real danger of losing life, or of suffering great bodily injury, or of losing important possessions, the latter often being as necessary as life or limb. According to the general opinion, a woman may kill an assailant when his death is necessary in defense of her chastity. 2. No other way of escape. 3. No direct intention of killing the aggressor, but only of defending one's self. 4. That no greater injury be intentionally inflicted than necessity requires. 5. That violence be used only when the danger is imminent.

Proof 1. Our right to live involves a right to use the means necessary for life, provided such means do not violate the rights of others. But, in the case of unjust aggression, the death of the aggressor may be the only means for saving one's life; nor are the rights of others thereby violated. Between the assailant and defendant arises a conflict of claims to life, in which, evidently, the right of the defendant prevails, while that of the assailant is suspended for the time being. The precedence of right belongs to the defendant, who has not willingly exposed himself to the danger, and is merely repelling an attack; but it cannot belong to the assailant, who is not acting from a motive of self-defense, and can cease from the attack or could have abstained from beginning it.

Proof 2. The thesis is a dictate of common sense, as Cicero declares in his plea for Milo.

164. **Objections.**

1. The end never justifies the means. *Answer.* The means employed in self-defense are not evil; the defendant intends by his physical act, which is not in itself evil, not the death of his aggressor, but his own defense, and he violates no rights.
2. God's right as master of life and death is violated. *Answer.* It is violated by the aggressor, who forces the defendant to strike the deadly blow.
3. We must love our enemies. *Answer.* Well ordered charity does not require us to love our enemies more than we love ourselves, nor even to love them with equal intensity.
4. But, if this last principle is true, we should be bound in duty to kill the aggressor; yet this doctrine is repugnant to charity. *Answer.* We are obliged to employ only ordinary means for the preservation of life. As homicide is certainly an extraordinary means, we are not obliged to make use of it, although we have a

right to do so. A man may waive this right, unless held back by imperative duties to others, and prefer, by a heroic act of charity, to lose his life rather than cut off his assailant while the latter has all his sins upon his head.

5. The foregoing does not apply, if the aggressor is an insane person. *Answer.* Though not an unjust aggressor formally, yet he is such materially. Hence the common opinion is that, in most cases, the killing, in self-defense, of an insane person is not against the natural law.

6. Then infanticide is not wrong, if it is necessary to save the mother's life. *Answer.* The unborn child is not an unjust aggressor, either formally or materially. Hence, the right of the mother who has caused, in some sense, the conflict of claims to life, must yield to the right of the child.

ARTICLE IV. DUTIES RELATING TO THE HONOR OF OTHERS.

165. **Honor** is the esteem in which a man is held by his fellow-men. Considered radically, or in its cause, it is a man's real excellence. Since all men have naturally, as beings endowed with rational faculties and destined for an exalted end, a certain high excellence, all men are naturally entitled to a certain honor. Still, as all men are not gifted with equal excellence, they are not all entitled to equal honor. A person may lose some of his claims to be honored or respected by others. It may be necessary for the common good, or even for some considerable private good, that the vices of an individual be exposed and his honor thus lessened.

Honor is unjustly impaired by: 1. *Insult*, or contumely, consisting in open, deliberate expressions of contempt; 2. *Calumny*, or false accusation; 3. *Detraction*, or the disclosure of another's secret faults to any one who has not a right to know them. The last two faults are still further specified as offenses against another's *good name*.

166. **Thesis XII.** *It is unlawful to impair another's honor, and necessary to make amends for its violation.*

Proof. We are obliged to love others as we love ourselves; but to lessen another's honor is not to love him as we love ourselves, for we would not have others do this unto us. We wish our honor to be respected, (a) as something valuable for its own sake and prized as such by noble minds; (b) as a protection of our rights, for a man in bad repute is more apt to suffer wrong and has little if any influence towards conciliating favor.

A man is obliged to make good the damage or loss which he has caused to another's honor or good name. Since justice demands that every one shall have his due, the honor unjustly taken away is due to him from whom it has been taken and must, as far as is possible, be restored.

167. **Duelling**, a practice handed down from the paganism of northern Europe, was once extensively used as a means for protecting or recovering personal honor. Happily, it has fallen into contempt and consequent disuse.

168. **Thesis XIV.** *Duelling is opposed to the natural law.*

Proof. A duel is a fight between two parties with murderous weapons, undertaken by private authority and according to previous appointment. Now, such an act is intrinsically wrong, and therefore opposed to the natural law. The act is intrinsically wrong, because it has the malice both of suicide and of murder. 1. A principal in a duel exposes his life without a just and reasonable cause, and he does this deliberately and by pre-arrangement. 2. He deliberately seeks the life of a fellow-man on his own private authority and without being forced by necessary self-defense.

169. **Objections.**
1. David is praised for his duel with Goliath. *Answer.* A single combat, authorized by the civil power as a means of warfare, is not a duel in the sense here attached to the word.
2. A duel may be necessary to avoid the imputation of cowardice. *Answer.* It would be moral cowardice to do a wrong action through human respect.
3. It is lawful to slay the unjust assailant of a man's honor, since many value honor more highly than life. *Answer.* Life can sometimes be defended only by striking down the unjust aggressor; but this is not true of a man's honor or good name. Moreover, the esteem in which one man is held by others is not more precious than life, though this is true of honor considered radically or in its cause, *i. e.*, personal excellence and virtue.
4. According to the general opinion, a woman may kill the assailant of her honor, or virtue, if there be no other means of escape. *Answer.* Honor in this case means more than a good name; it means bodily chastity, which its owner has a right to defend as a priceless possession (No. 163, 1).

CHAPTER V.

RIGHTS OF OWNERSHIP IN MATERIAL PROPERTY.

170. **Ownership** is the right to dispose of property at will, and to exclude others from its use. By property, we mean the external material goods of the earth, which men can divide amongst themselves.

ARTICLE I. VALIDITY OF TITLES TO OWNERSHIP.

171. **Thesis XV.** *We have a right to own property.*

Explanation. The ownership here spoken of is not absolute: it is dependent on God.

Proof. We have a right to live, indeed we are bound by duty to our Creator to preserve our lives; hence we have a natural right to the means necessary to preserve life. But the ownership of property, *i. e.*, the holding, using, and disposing at will of material goods to the exclusion of other men, is a necessary means for the preservation of life. Therefore, we have a right to own property.

172. **Thesis XVI.** *We have the right to increase or lay up property.*

Proof 1. Our right to life not only exists for the present hour or day, but it also extends into the future; hence we have the right to the ordinary means for prolonging our lives by providing betimes for future wants, such as sickness, old age, or the dependence upon us of other persons. Now, this implies a right to increase our property beyond present needs. Therefore, we have a right to increase or lay up property.

Proof 2. All men, considered specifically, or according to their common nature, are equal; therefore, no one is bound either to labor for another or to surrender the results of his labor without just compensation. Yet this a man would be forced to do, unless rights to property were lasting; because, if a claim to property had been established, and that claim could not continue, the labor which the claimant had expended in obtaining or developing the property would pass without compensation to another man.

173. The principles explained in the preceding paragraphs apply to **landed property** just as well as to other material goods of a less stable character. Yet the right of private individuals to own land has been, of late years especially, vigorously denied, as unjust and opposed to the natural law. This doctrine, or land theory, has had for its most prominent champion in our own country Mr. Henry George, who declares (Progress and Poverty, B. VI., C. II.) that private ownership in land is the chief source "of the unjust and unequal distribution of wealth apparent in modern civilization." He finds only one remedy: "We must make land common property." His reasonings are as ingenious as his claim is bold and his language forcible; but they are full of sophistry. He begins by granting that if the remedy is a true one it must be consistent with justice. But he fails in his earnest attempt to prove this for his land theory. In striving to establish the justice of his claim, he does not hold the teaching of the Communists that any kind of private property is unlawful. On the contrary, he refutes this teaching with much ability and force. "What constitutes," he asks (B.

VII., C. I.), "the rightful basis of property? What is it that enables a man to justly say of a thing, 'It is mine'? From what springs the sentiment which acknowledges his exclusive right as against all the world? Is it not primarily the right of a man to himself, to the use of his own powers, to the enjoyment of the fruits of his own exertions? Is it not this individual right which springs from and is testified to by the natural facts of individual organization—the fact that each particular pair of hands obey a particular brain and are related to a particular stomach; the fact that each man is a definite, coherent, and independent whole—which alone justifies individual ownership? As a man belongs to himself, so his labor when put in concrete form belongs to him.

"And for this reason, that which a man makes or produces is his own, as against the world—to enjoy or to destroy, to use, to exchange, or to give. No one else can rightfully claim it, and his exclusive right to it involves no wrong to anyone else. Thus there is to everything produced by human exertion a clear and indisputable title to exclusive possession and enjoyment, which is perfectly consistent with justice, as it descended from the original producer in whom it vested by natural law. The pen with which I am writing is justly mine. No other human being can rightfully lay claim to it, for in me is the title of the producer who made it. It has become mine because transferred to me by the stationer, to whom it was transferred by the importer, who obtained the exclusive right to it by transfer from the manufacturer, in whom by the same process of purchase vested the rights of those who dug the material from the ground and shaped it into a pen. Thus my exclusive right of ownership in the pen springs from the natural right of the individual to the use of his own faculties."

The theory, however, proves too much. If the principle were true that right to ownership can be established only by transforming labor, man could own nothing, for he can produce nothing without material to work upon. The iron or gold of which the pen is made is not produced by man; hence, in the very first instance, appropriation by occupation must be admitted as a true title to the raw material. Mr. George is, therefore, entirely mistaken when he goes on to say: "There can be to the ownership of anything no rightful title which is not derived from the title of the producer." In his elaborate development of this false proposition, on which his theory of the injustice of private ownership in land chiefly rests, the same fallacy is ever recurring, namely, the confusion of *production* with any exercise of the human faculties. The explorer does not produce the desert land which he discovers; and yet he acquires a clear title to it on Mr. George's own principle that he exerts his faculties in its acquisition. Mr. George's theory is, therefore, unsound; he totally fails to prove the injustice of private ownership in land. His attacks on land owners are not justified, and are consequently unwise. For, as he himself says: "That alone is wise which is just, that alone is enduring which is right."

174. **Thesis XVIII.** *Mere first occupancy is by itself a valid title to ownership.*

Explanation. Occupation consists in taking possession of something that does not belong to another person, and that can be an object of ownership. This means of acquiring ownership can be employed at present to only a very limited extent, since land and nearly all movable property belong to individuals, or companies, or governments.

Proof. The principle that a man is entitled to possess

what he first occupies, provided it be the property of no other person, is universally admitted as a dictate of common sense. The only thing opposed to it is the doctrine of Communism, that all goods are by nature positively common to all men. But this doctrine is absurd, for a man would be thereby made slavishly dependent upon all other men, without whose permission he could not justly appropriate anything for his personal use. The child or the man, savage or civilized, that catches a wild fowl or fish, that finds a valuable stone belonging to no one, that gathers wild fruit, will justly claim ownership as a right by priority of possession. There is no reason why this principle should apply to movable goods only and not to land as well, provided he who finds a piece of land ownerless marks it by some external sign as his property, thus indicating his intention of keeping it and of excluding all others from the possession of it.

175. **In modern times** occupancy of a new land is effected by some state or government, which thus becomes the first owner. Next, individuals acquire possession by complying with certain conditions determined by the civil power. In this country, lands are held in virtue of original grants made either by the United States directly, or by other governments that controlled tracts which afterward came under the jurisdiction of the United States. These latter grants were confirmed later on by the present government. Once the conditions placed by the civil power are complied with by the occupants, their rights are fixed, and both justice and the common good demand that they be kept inviolable. The Constitution of the United States provides that no private property shall be taken for public uses without just compensation. In this, the Constitution only enunciates the natural right of private owners; and therefore no amendment of the Consti-

tution could ever confer upon the government the right freely to confiscate the land.

176. Yet a state might hold landed property in common, as was done to some extent among the Irish clans, and later on in the French Colony of Louisiana. But, as a rule, it is far more expedient to encourage private industry by allotting portions of the land to private persons, or permitting them to take possession according to certain formalities that the State will determine for the common good. Nearly all nations have, in their early history, acted on these principles; and thus the division of land by occupancy, yet with public sanction and according to public regulations, is said to have been made **jure gentium**. This term does not mean *international law*, but *the law of the nations* in this sense, that it is the prevalent legislation of all nations in accordance with the exigencies of natural rights.

177. The state retains two restrictions on private ownership, founded on the requirements of the common good: 1. The right of **taxation**, that is, the imposition of a burden proportionate to the protection bestowed, and not any tax at will; for justice requires a proportion between what is given and what is received. 2. The right of **eminent domain**, *i. e.*, the right of taking private property for public uses when necessary, with compensation made to the owners.

178. **Thesis XIX.** *A grant of unoccupied land, made by civil society to private parties, on proper conditions, founds a just claim to ownership.*

Proof 1. Society can make such laws as promote its end—the general welfare of the community—provided it does not violate any prior rights. But such assignments, or grants, made on proper conditions, contribute to the general welfare and violate no prior rights. For such a measure promotes enterprise, industry, and public spirit, without which a high degree of civilization would be difficult, if not impossible.

Proof 2. A State can dispose of its property for the common good. This it does by allotting lands as a reward to soldiers who have fought for their country, or for the purpose of encouraging settlers to clear and improve the ground, or as an inducement to corporations to make roads, build bridges and other public works, and thus open up the country to trade and travel.

179. **Thesis XX.** *Communism and Socialism are unjust and injurious.*

Explanation. Communism denies the right of private ownership and declares that all property is by nature positively common. Socialism demands that all productive property shall be given over to the State, which would thus become sole proprietor of land, manufactories, railroads, etc., and sole distributor of the compensation due to every individual member of the commonwealth for his labor. Now we maintain that Communism and Socialism, if introduced as general systems in the present order of things, would be unjust and injurious.

Proof. The fundamental principle of Communism is false, namely, that by nature all goods were intended for mankind to be *positively* common, so that no one could justly appropriate to himself anything beyond immediate pressing wants, without the consent of the other members of the community. The absurdity of this view is manifest from the unnatural dependence in which man would be thereby placed. Another false principle made use of by both systems is the absolute and entire equality of all men. In the abstract and before the law, all men are said to be equal; but in the *concrete*, no two men are exactly equal. No two men have equal powers of body and mind, equal abilities for government or trade, the same tastes and dispositions, even the same rational wants.

Both systems would begin by depriving men of the fruit of past labors; both would confiscate the earnings of one man for the benefit of others without compensation, thus violating a great natural right. Moreover, it is impossible for either system, judged on economic grounds, to last, or to attain even a fraction of the fanciful plenty so freely promised by its advocates. The latter seem to base their calculations on the utopian dream, that, in the new Communistic or Socialistic Republic, men shall lose their selfishness and be free from their passions, and will freely practise heroic self-denial and self-forgetfulness; that, in other words, men shall be transformed into angels. Yet these same leaders generally ignore or repudiate religion, the wellspring of self-sacrifice, and aim at sweeping away the rights of Church and family.

ARTICLE II. VIOLATIONS OF OWNERSHIP.

180. The violation of the right of ownership, if committed secretly, is called **theft**; it is called **robbery**, if the act is done openly and with physical force. Such violations disturb the balance of equality which justice demands for all the members of the community. The balance cannot be properly restored except by the **restitution** of the property unjustly acquired. What was stolen continues to belong to the one from whom it was taken, and must be given back to him. *Res clamat ad dominum*, "property calls for its owner," is an important axiom of jurisprudence. Even if the owner cannot be found, it is not fair that the thief should retain what he has stolen: *fraus sua nemini patrocinari debet*, "no one

should reap any benefit from his fraud." He must part with his ill-gotten goods, disposing of them as he may presume the owner would direct, if he could be consulted; for instance, by giving them or their value to the poor.

181. If damage has been done willfully to the property of another, **reparation of the damage** must be made before equality can be restored. This duty rests, in the first place, upon the chief perpetrator of the damage; and, secondarily, upon those who have voluntarily aided him, physically or morally, to inflict the injury. Such aid or co-operation may be given in various ways, viz.: by taking part in the material action; by command, advice, consent; by sheltering or concealing; by sharing in ill-gotten gains; and even by not warning, not preventing, or not making the guilty known when one is, in justice, bound to do so.

ARTICLE III. VARIOUS MODES OF ACQUIRING PROPERTY.

182. **The chief modes of acquiring property** are the following:

1. **First occupancy**: that is, taking possession of any material object that is really without an owner. (No. 174.) Domestic animals, even when they have strayed far from their owner, remain his property; but wild animals, though captured and tamed, if once they have regained their native liberty, are considered as belonging to no one till captured again, when they become the property of their new captor.

2. **The finding of lost articles.** These have an owner to whom they must be returned, if he can be discovered with reasonable effort. If, however, the owner

cannot be discovered, the articles become the property of the finder. When hidden treasures of great value are found in civilized lands, their ownership or apportionment is settled according to existing laws that have been enacted for such cases. The goods of those who die intestate, and without natural heirs, are to be disposed of as the laws direct.

3. **Accession** is a title to new property that is added to my former possessions, either naturally, *e. g.*, by birth, as with the young of cattle, or by alluvion, as by deposits of soil on a river bank; or accidentally, or even designedly, as when another plants or builds on my grounds, or in other ways improves my property. In these instances, disputed claims may arise which the civil law is to decide.

4. **Prescription** is a title to ownership of property based on the fact that it has been held in quiet and *bona fide* possession for the space of time appointed by the law. This supposes: 1. That the property is such as can be lawfully acquired by a private person. 2. That the person in possession has honestly considered it all along as his property. 3. That he has remained in undisputed and uninterrupted possession during the required time.

The common good demands that claims to property reaching back beyond a reasonable period should be disregarded, in order that ownership may be settled on a solid basis.

ARTICLE IV. THE TRANSFER OF PROPERTY BY CONTRACT.

183. Ownership has been defined (No. 170) to be the right to dispose at will of material, external goods. Now, the right to dispose of an object at will involves the right to transfer it to another person. This act of transfer begins in the owner's will, is continued in the expression to the other party of this act of his will, and is completed by the latter's acceptance of the offer. This consent, externally manifested, of the two parties concerned, agreeing to the transfer of rights, is called a **contract.**

184. A contract is **gratuitous,** or one-sided, if only one party gives up a right to ownership, the other party accepting the proffered benefit without any cost to himself. This is the case in free gifts amongst the living or in the behests of the dying. In either instance, the equality implied in natural justice requires the person benefited to make the compensation of gratitude to the donor.

185. A man has a right, derived not from civil legislation but from the natural law, to dispose of his property by his **last will.** Yet he cannot do it in such a manner as to violate the rights and just claims of others. Hence, the father of a family has no right to alienate his entire property in favor of externs, if in so doing he should leave his wife and children destitute. If he dies without making a will, they have a right, founded on the natural law, to inherit his property. The share that each member of the family shall receive is usually determined by existing civil laws.

186. **Inviolability is due to last wills,** not only by reason of the right which the testator has to dispose of his property, but also on account of the common good of society. Few men would care to exert themselves beyond the efforts

necessary for present needs, if they could not dispose of the property acquired by their toil for the benefit, after their death, of those who are nearest and dearest to them, or of objects and institutions the success and continuity of which they had greatly at heart during life.

187. All contracts in which both parties assume an obligation, or in which both yield some right for the benefit received, are called **onerous.** The rights thus exchanged or transferred need not be those of ownership; yet, of whatever kind they may be, the principle of equality between what is given and what is received determines the justice of the transaction. This principle, however, is not to be too strictly interpreted. If, for example, I take a fancy to an article of little intrinsic value in the possession of another and induce him to let me have it at a high price, the bargain is just. Though *materially* no equality exists between the price and the thing purchased, still there may be an equality *formally* between what I pay and the value that, of my own free choice, I set on the article. But this supposes that the excess of the price is assented to freely on my part. If another takes advantage of my special need and forces me to pay more than the commodity is worth, he does me an injustice, and the contract is unjust.

188. To be valid or binding, every contract, whether it be gratuitous or onerous, **must be attended with the following conditions:**

> 1. The contracting parties must be *competent persons*— *i. e.*, in the full possession of reason; hence, infants, insane and intoxicated persons are not competent; minors are legally incompetent—*i. e.*, their contracts are usually not recognized as valid before the law.
>
> 2. The *matter* of the contract must be *appropriate*—

i. e., the rights transferred must be really capable of transference, and must belong to those who exchange them. Hence, no one can validly bargain to do a thing that he has no right to do.

3. *Proper form* must be observed. Both civil and ecclesiastical authority may, each in its own province, appoint certain forms, the non-observance of which renders some contracts null and void. The natural form essential to every contract is the true, full and mutual consent of the contracting parties. This supposes that both have a sufficient knowledge of what they are agreeing to. Hence, if one of the parties seriously misunderstands the contract, he is not bound to stand by it. Contracts made by minors can frequently be rescinded or annulled by their parents or guardians, because minors are supposed to act with insufficient knowledge.

ARTICLE V. THE WAGES OF LABORERS.

189. The relations between laborers and their employers ought to be such as to conduce to the benefit of both parties. This cannot be the case unless full justice be done on each side. It is therefore of great importance to understand in this matter the golden mean between the exactions of grinding capitalists and the unreasonable demands of Communists and Socialists.

By **wages,** we understand the compensation agreed upon by the workman and his employer for the former's services to the latter. We shall first consider such an agreement merely as an onerous contract, money or its equivalent being exchanged for work. Each party has a right to that which he gives in exchange; and if the compensation is proportionate to the services rendered, the contract is just. The services thus contracted for cannot be of use to the employer, as productive property, except in their results. Accordingly, whatever profit he can derive by the combination and direction of such labor above that which the wage-earners themselves could have won by their individual exertions is his gain; whatever he loses thereby is his loss. They have no part in the management; consequently, it would be unreasonable for the laborers to claim, in addition to the stipulated compensation, the right to divide with their employer the profits of his management.

Their mutual relations—we are not speaking of co-operative associations—are not those of partnership; else the losses, as well as the profits, would have to be shared in common.

190. How shall we determine the **proper amount of wages to be paid to each laborer?** The answer to this question is not easy, especially for particular cases. The following principles, however, are of general application:

1. To preserve the balance of equality, which ought to exist in every onerous contract, between what is given and what is received in return, a laborer who, by *superior skill or industry*, renders more valuable service than others, is entitled to higher wages.
2. The laborer who is called upon to expend *unusual exertion*, by performing more painful or more protracted toil, by exposing life or limb or health to more than ordinary danger, by devoting an uncommonly long time to the task of preparing and qualifying himself for his position, is entitled to a compensation exceeding the ordinary wages.
3. The chief difficulty is encountered in fixing the

amount of wages for *ordinary service*. This must be the standard or basis of wages. For other kinds of service there ought to be higher pay; but what shall we give for ordinary service? Labor, many answer, is like merchandise, and its owner, the laborer, is entitled to that only which his labor will bring in the market; and hence, whatever he agrees to accept, even though forced by stress of need or competition to sell his toil for a pittance, that is the proper amount. Now, this view is erroneous and unjust. Labor is not common merchandise; it is the wear and tear of life in rational beings, every one of whom has an inalienable right to his life—not the life of a beast of burden, but the life of a man. Hence, he has the right to all that is necessary to maintain *human* life, not only in his own person, but also in those who are naturally dependent upon him for the means of subsistence. The wages, therefore, which an employer is bound in justice to pay to the man that labors for his interest as faithfully as a human being can be fairly expected to labor, ought to be sufficient to support the workman and his wife and children with decency and reasonable comfort. This is the **minimum quantity of wages.**[*]

[*] "The labor of the working-man is not only his personal attribute, but it is necessary; and this makes all the difference: the preservation of life is the bounden duty of each and all, and to fail therein is a crime. It follows that each has a right to procure what is required in order to live; and the poor can procure it in no other way than by work and wages. Let it be granted, then, that, as a rule, workmen and employer should make free agreements, and, in particular, should freely agree as to wages; nevertheless, there is a dictate of nature more imperious and more ancient than any bargain between man and man, viz., that the remuneration must be enough to support the wage-earner in reasonable and frugal comfort. If, through necessity or fear of a worse evil, the workman accepts harder conditions because an employer or a contractor will give him no better, he is the victim of force and injustice."—Pope Leo XIII., Encyclical on Labor, 1891.

191. Can wage-earners justly form organizations to protect themselves against exacting capitalists?—in other words, are **labor unions** lawful? A right to an end implies a right to the means necessary to attain that end, if such means do not violate the rights of others. Now, laborers have a right to fair wages; therefore, they have a right to the just means necessary to obtain fair wages. But organized association on the part of workingmen is often necessary; it is often the only means of securing fair wages from overreaching employers. Such association does injustice to no one. Therefore, workingmen can, with justice, have recourse to labor unions as a means of self-protection.

Are **strikes** illicit? Men have a right to refuse working for unfair wages. Their places may be taken by others, and the latter cannot justly be prevented from doing so, except by moral suasion. Of course, employers also have a right to form unions, in order to protect themselves against unreasonable demands of their employees.

192. If the common good is injured by the general stoppage of work attendant on strikes and lock-outs, the **most proper remedy** is to be sought in the intercession and arbitration of fair-minded and disinterested persons. On general principles, it is not desirable that the government should meddle with peaceful disputes of citizens, as long as private means are at hand for bringing about a good understanding. Boards of arbitration are usually the best agency for restoring health and vigor to the whole industrial system.*

* "In these and similar questions, however, such as, for example, the hours of labor in different trades, the sanitary precautions to be observed in factories, workshops, etc., in order to supersede undue interference on the part of the state, especially as circumstances, times and localities differ so widely, it is advisable that recourse be had to societies or boards, . . . or to some other method of safeguarding the interests of wage-earners, the state to be asked for approval and protection."—Leo XIII., Encyclical on Labor.

Yet no general or lasting cure can be effected, except by animating the members of both classes with the spirit of justice and mutual love. Now, this cannot be secured without a sound education, which itself implies the doctrines of the true religion.

BOOK III.

SOCIAL RIGHTS AND DUTIES.

CHAPTER I.

SOCIETY IN GENERAL.

193. Men, we know from observation, are not by nature isolated individuals. They are associated in many ways: as members of families, as belonging to a tribe, as dwelling close to one another in hamlets and towns, as fellow-citizens of a political State. This relation of men to one another gives rise to a most important class of rights and duties, which we shall study in the present book.

A **society** is *the union of several or many persons for the purpose of obtaining a common end by the use of common means.* Sociality, in the strict meaning of the term, is distinctive of man, since only rational beings can direct means to an end. Brutes can never be social, though they may sometimes be gregarious; some species may simulate society by instinctively acting in concert for a common good.

194. The nature of each society is specified by the end for which it was established. *Religious* society, the noblest of societies, because its end is noblest, promotes the worship of God; *domestic* society was instituted for the sake

of family life; the end of *civil* society is the welfare of the nation; *international* society forwards the prosperity of many nations bound together for the protection of their common interests. Besides, there are innumerable societies of less importance than the far-reaching associations mentioned above, such as benevolent, commercial, literary and scientific societies. It need hardly be mentioned that no society is lawful that is detrimental to the common good, or to the welfare of a higher society.

195. We may ascertain **the rights of any society** in particular by examining the end for which it exists. If the end is lawful, the means to that end are lawful, provided such means violate no prior right. Hence, an obvious right of a society is to direct its members in the use of the proper means. Moreover, since the society is either necessary for the members or is entered of their own free will, it has the right to enforce upon its members the use of the common means.

196. **Thesis I.** *Authority is necessary to society.*

Proof. Authority is the *moral power of directing men's conduct and of enforcing such direction.* Now, such a power is necessary for the end of society. For the members must often be informed regarding the nature of their duties and the manner of performing them; men are free and are naturally inclined to seek their own individual advantage, often to the detriment of the common good; they may sometimes find it advances their own selfish interests to hinder others from performing their duty. Hence, unless a society has the power to direct its members and to enforce such direction, it cannot attain its end.

197. From these explanations it is clear that authority is to be exercised only for the good of the society. **The**

Society in General. 121

office of a person in authority is a public trust, and not merely a personal privilege; it demands, therefore, prudence and fidelity. The extent of his authority depends upon the nature of his trust, and the importance of the end and of the several means required to attain the end. The application of compulsion beyond just limits is called *tyranny*.

198. All mankind constitute a universal society, of which God Himself is the founder, ruler, law-giver, and judge. This universal association fills all the requirements of a society (No. 193): it is (*a*) a union of rational beings placed here upon earth, (*b*) for the common purpose of rendering glory to God and securing their own eternal happiness, (*c*) which purpose is to be accomplished by the observance of the same natural law under the authority of the one Supreme Law-giver.

199. **Thesis II.** *Society is natural to man, and therefore the institution of God.*

Proof 1. The constant and universal fact of human society must have a proportionate cause, which can be no other than the human nature which God has given to each and every man. Moreover, the need which all men have of assistance from other persons in order to attain the end of their existence is an unmistakable sign that this need or exigency of human society is natural to all men, and consequently has been implanted in human nature by the Sovereign Author of nature.

> 1. The infant needs its parents for its very existence and for the preservation of its life.
> 2. The child must be sustained and educated by others.
> 3. The youth requires the guidance and control of maturer minds.

4. The full-grown man and woman generally need each other's assistance to lead a life of intelligence and comfort, of mutual love and abiding happiness.

5. Old age would be miserable indeed without the support and love of a younger generation.

Proof 2. Man's higher powers, his splendid faculties of intellect and will, were surely not bestowed upon him to lie dormant and neglected, but to be developed and put to use. Now, even if man could, unassisted by his fellows, preserve his life against wild beasts and the elements, yet without the society of other men he could rise only a little above idiocy. Long and intimate association with polished minds is indispensable for advance in the sciences and arts. Besides, in the normal state of things, man's wonderful powers of speech and hearing make society a necessary element of human happiness.

Proof 3. Some of man's noblest tendencies, which were certainly given to him for a purpose, find no exercise except in human society; such are benevolence, pity for the unfortunate, admiration of virtue and of heroism, self-devotion to the common good, and similar dispositions, which are called the social virtues. Nor will the general society of human kind afford proper play for these tendencies; a closer association in particular societies is evidently required, in which mutual example and encouragement incite to generous deeds of self-sacrifice and of devotion to a great cause.

CHAPTER II.

DOMESTIC SOCIETY.

ARTICLE I. THE NATURE AND PURPOSE OF DOMESTIC SOCIETY.

200. The form of society most ancient and most necessary for the human race is the family or domestic society. It originates in **marriage**, which is defined to be: The union of a man and a woman, involving their living together in undivided intercourse. Marriage is the institution of the Creator Himself. He made woman to be man's companion, not his slave—"A help like unto himself" (Gen. ii. 18). The qualities of the two sexes were not to be identical, but to be similar and supplementary; wisdom, strength, and firmness predominating on the one side, deference and tenderness on the other; while mutual love and fidelity were to join both parties in the one indissoluble union of wedlock: "Wherefore a man shall leave his father and mother and shall cleave to his wife, and they shall be two in one flesh" (Gen. ii. 24).

201. **The primary ends of marriage** are the generation and education of children, whereby the human race is perpetuated and elevated to a becoming standard of intellectual and moral excellence.

    1. This perpetuation of the race is evidently intended by the Creator, who not only bade our first parents "increase and multiply and fill the earth" (Gen. i.

28), but He also implanted in the natures of men and women such inclinations and needs that this design can never be frustrated.

2. Yet it is not necessary for this purpose that every one shall enter the state of marriage; but exceptions in this matter may be expedient, even apart from supernatural considerations.

The intellectual and moral elevation of mankind is far more important than its numerical increase. This principle has been acted upon by countless heroes of all times, who have sacrificed their lives in youth or vigorous manhood for the advance of truth and science, for the honor and liberty of their country, or for the spread of civilization. An army is highly benefited by the presence of magnanimous leaders; mankind likewise is elevated by the example of intrepid souls, and particularly of those who sacrifice for a great religious motive the pleasures and comforts of marriage and lead a life of perpetual continency. In this career, the most perfect among the sons of men has set Himself as the pattern, and millions have followed His example. However much the low-minded and sensual may sneer at such a practice or deny the possibility of its long continuance, the experience of God's saints and innumerable chosen souls makes it manifest that such a life is possible, and, with special supernatural graces, comparatively easy.

202. **The secondary end** of marriage is the direct good of the contracting parties, their peace, mutual love, and union of mind and heart. This condition of things results partly from similarity of tastes and dispositions; but it depends chiefly upon the practice of the social virtues, especially of an enduring conjugal love, by which each party is prompted to further the happiness of the other. Yet in its primary and

secondary ends, marriage is subordinate to the last end of man, his everlasting beatitude.

ARTICLE II. THE UNITY AND INDISSOLUBILITY OF MARRIAGE.

203. The two chief properties of marriage are **unity** and **indissolubility**. One man and one woman are joined in wedlock, promising, as the old formula correctly expresses it, to take each other as husband and wife, "for better, for worse, for richer, for poorer, in sickness and health, till death do us part." To the unity of marriage are opposed *polyandry*, or plurality of husbands, and *polygamy*, or the plurality of wives. To indissolubility is opposed *divorce*.

204. **Polyandry** is destructive of the very idea of order in domestic society, because, if man is to retain his natural headship of the family, it would give several heads to the same family. Besides, polyandry defeats both the primary and the secondary ends of marriage. Even if in this condition of affairs children were born, it would be very difficult, if not impossible, to tell who was the father of each particular child, so that the education of such practically fatherless offspring would be incomplete and neglected. And can we imagine that domestic peace and love could find place in such a household? Consequently, polyandry is entirely opposed to the natural law.

205. **Polygamy**, though it does not make the generation and education of the children impossible, is directly opposed to the secondary end of marriage, for it is the unfailing cause of jealousy, strife and domestic unhappiness; it degrades woman from her true rank to the condition of slavery. Hence, polygamy is a violation of the natural law, though

not to so great an extent as polyandry. History shows that polygamous nations have advanced very slowly, if at all, in civilization, and that amongst them the increase of population has not equaled that of monogamous nations.

To the objection that God permitted polygamy to the patriarchs of old, we answer that God never approved the practice. He tolerated it for a period, until, in the fullness of time, His holy will was more luminously declared, and the original unity of marriage was re-established. Even if God did allow plurality of wives in past ages, it does not follow that the practice may be adopted without His special dispensation. He alone controls the rights of all parties, and He alone could prevent the evils that must result naturally from a polygamous union.

206. **Indissolubility** is the second property of marriage, that is, the marriage contract is of such a nature, that, once entered upon, it continues in force until the death of one of the contracting parties. A lasting union it was meant to be from the beginning: " Wherefore a man shall leave his father and mother and shall cleave to his wife" (Gen. ii. 24). This property is violated by **divorce**, which consists in annulling or breaking the marriage contract, so that each of the contracting parties may marry again during the lifetime of the other.

Divorce is opposed to one of the primary objects of marriage, namely, the proper education of the children. The latter have a natural right to the support, the supervision, the good example, the abiding love of both their parents, to whom, in return, they owe lasting reverence, love, and gratitude. Yet these duties, which are established by the natural law, divorce makes impossible of fulfillment. It turns the mutual love of husband and wife into mutual hatred; the children cannot cling to both parents, and thence results a house divided against itself, a byword of disgrace.

Moreover, if divorce were foreseen as possible, how easily would mutual distrust be aroused, to be followed by domestic discord. "If," says the Rev. Joseph Rickaby, S. J. (Moral Philosophy, p. 276), "a divorce *a vinculo* were a visible object on the matrimonial horizon, the parties would be strongly encouraged thereby to form illicit connections, in their expectation of having any one of them ratified and sanctified by marriage. Marriage would be entered upon lightly, as a thing easily to be done and readily undone, a state of things not very far in advance of promiscuity."

207. It is sometimes objected that the unnatural conduct of one of the contracting parties may make the continuation of family life a moral impossibility, and that in this case divorce is the less of two evils. Such a state of affairs may indeed render it impossible for the parties in question to live together; nevertheless divorce is not therefore admissible. An escape from the difficulty may be had, without violation of law or of right, by a **temporary separation**, *a toro*, "from bed and board," as the arrangement is termed, which may be indefinitely prolonged according to need. Yet this measure differs from a separation *a vinculo*, or the annulment of the marriage contract. Among baptized Christians, for whom marriage is a sacrament figuring the spotless and irrevocable espousals of the Son of God with His Church, every valid marriage that has been consummated is absolutely incapable of annulment: "What God has joined together, let no man put asunder" (Matt. xix. 6).

208. Marriage is, therefore, by its nature, a bond that can be loosened only by death. It may be asked **whether divorce is essentially wrong**, *i. e.*, whether it is so opposed to the

natural law as to be inadmissible under any conditions. We know that in the time of the Old Testament, God allowed or tolerated it for some special cases in the midst of general corruption. But toleration of a measure is immensely different from approval of the same. Besides, it is one thing for God, the Sovereign Master and Guardian of rights, to dispense from a law, and quite another thing for the civil authorities to grant a similar dispensation in a matter that does not come within their jurisdiction. The civil powers do not create the family, nor can they without injustice bring about its destruction.

209. **Thesis III.** *The rights of domestic society are not derived from civil society.*

Explanation. To Catholics it is evident that civil society cannot without sacrilege usurp control over matrimony, which is a sacrament instituted by Christ. But we are here considering the subject in the light of natural reason, prescinding from the special dignity to which we know by Revelation the marriage contract has been elevated.

Proof 1. The individuals composing a State must have existence before the State can exist, and these individuals have, by their nature, the right to form domestic society. Add to this, the institution of marriage and the entire constitution of the family are antecedent, historically, to the formation of civil society. Consequently, the rights of the family cannot be derived from civil society; and therefore the latter can advance no title to control or modify rights which it did not originate.

Proof 2. Every rightly constituted society can justly claim only such powers as are necessary for the attainment of its own distinctive end, and it can claim no powers that infringe upon prior rights. But to attain its ends—the public peace and the protection of personal rights—the State has no need of jurisdiction over marriage, the education of children, or other matters pertaining naturally to the family or the individual, and this, too, by a right prior to the rights of the State. On the contrary, by depriving individuals or families of their natural rights, which it is bound to protect, civil society contradicts its own end.

Proof 3. A nobler society cannot be subject in the matter of its inherent and distinctive rights to a society that is less noble. But domestic society is nobler in its ends and object than civil society, and therefore cannot be subject to the latter in the matter of its essential rights. The end of domestic society is the propagation, and, especially, the education of the human race for time and eternity, whilst the end of civil society is happiness in this world; hence, the advantages it secures are less intimately connected with the true happiness of men than those aimed at by domestic society.

210. **The State has a right** as the guardian of public decency to forbid such marriages as are opposed to the natural law. Though it can have no jurisdiction over the substantial features of marriage, it may assert control in the matter of certain external forms or accessories, in order to insure the protection of individual rights, such as the settlement of property and the rightful succession to titles and privileges. Hence the State may demand a record of valid marriages, and for this purpose may require compliance with legal formalities, *e. g.*, of registration, provided the burdens thus imposed be reasonable and for the common good. Should it be objected that the State has a right to regulate contracts, and, therefore, the marriage contract, we reply that the State has no right over contracts that are in their nature prior to its existence. In so far as civil consequences are involved in

family matters, the State is bound to protect natural rights, but it cannot create or control them. Except in cases of gross violation of strict rights among members of a family, the presumption is against State interference in the concerns of domestic society.

ARTICLE III. PARENTAL AUTHORITY. EDUCATION.

211. The temporal and eternal happiness of men, as well as the prosperity of civil society, depends chiefly, in the natural order, on the perfection of domestic society. Now an essential condition for the welfare of every society is a proper exercise of its authority; since in this manner the necessary means are directed to the end for which the society exists. Hence, in discussing principles of domestic society, we must first decide in whom the authority of the family resides.

Thesis IV. *The husband is naturally the head of the family.*

Proof 1. The universal practice of all races of men shows that this is a dictate of common sense.

Proof 2. He to whom the other members of the family look naturally for protection, support and direction, is intended by the Author of nature to possess authority in the family, or to be its head. Now, such a one, in the normal state of affairs, allowance being made for occasional and partial exceptions, is the husband, the father of the family. For (*a*) the husband is properly the founder of the family, the primary cause of its existence; woman was created to be a help and companion to man. (*b*) It is he who, as a rule, is expected to provide for the family its means of support. (*c*) On account of his superior strength of mind and body, all look to him for direction in doubt, and for defense in danger. (*d*) He is to represent the interests of the family abroad, the wife being detained at home habitually by duties which she can best perform. (*e*) Nature's gifts have been so divided between husband and wife that reason, which is the faculty for ruling, is more dominant in the former, love and sympathy in the latter. He is the head, and she the heart; but the head should direct the heart.

212. **The wife and mother**, who is not a menial, but the helpmate and companion of her husband, shares his parental dignity, and is likewise entitled to a share in his authority over the family. She is naturally the centre of domestic affection, the dispenser of the comforts provided by the father, the mistress of the home, subject indeed to his prudent direction when important occasions make such direction necessary, yet possessing the right to manage her own domain. From her lips the children will receive direction and warning, and her loving hand will correct their faults. The father will, if need be, firmly support her authority, and by word and example teach the children to venerate their mother.

213. **Education** is the most important duty of parents towards their offspring. It consists in the well-proportioned development of the child's faculties to prepare him to make efforts for himself in order to secure happiness in this world and the next. Bodily development is first in the order of time; moral and religious education is first in the order of importance; for religion and morality lead to the highest and most lasting happiness. Cultivation of the intellect in some degree is necessary for all men, though there can be no universal standard in this matter; the extent of the mental training to be given to the child must depend largely on the position in life which he may be reasonably expected to hold

in after years. Book-learning is not the measure of personal happiness or of public usefulness; but attainments in the moral order, whether they be accompanied with scholarship or not, are an unfailing source of happiness to their possessor and of valuable service to other men and to the State.

214. **Religion** is the most important element of education. The child has the right to be prepared for all the most important duties of life. Now, among these latter, the worship of God takes precedence of all others, and is to be most solicitously provided for. Nor can the principles of morality be inculcated without dogmatic religious teaching; for men will not observe the natural law unless they know that it has a proportionate sanction. But to teach the existence of such a sanction is to teach religion. All parents of sound judgment are constantly teaching their children principles of natural religion, and no one who possesses a sufficient understanding of this important subject, can honestly disagree with Washington's declaration: "Howsoever great the influence of a polite education is said to be on certain minds, reason and experience by no means allow us to expect that morality shall prevail in a nation if religious principles be excluded."

When, moreover, parents are blessed with supernatural truth and grace, they would be exceedingly cruel to their child if they denied him what they themselves consider to be the most precious and necessary possession on earth—the knowledge of God's revealed religion. Hence, the Christian education of their children is the most sacred duty of Christian parents.

215. Enemies of revealed religion have, especially in recent times, advocated an unreasonable system of education, which recalls the harsh and unnatural training in vogue

amongst the ancient Spartans—namely, **State control of education.** They maintain that the State should assume the office of educating the young without regard for the natural rights of parents. By this means, the youth of the land could be imbued with the political principles of the ruling power or party, and, especially, they could be indoctrinated with irreligion and be induced to look with complete indifference, if not with abhorrence, upon the Faith of their ancestors. This system finds favor with certain political writers and leaders who aim at extending and centralizing the civil power; with self-seeking demagogues who scheme for a control of patronage in the system of State education; with Socialists who would destroy individual liberty and make the State all-powerful; and with many well-meaning, though deluded men who, not perceiving the wrong and the danger of such a course, prefer State control of education as a cheaper and less troublesome method, and even as a safeguard against what they fancy to be the subversion by the Catholic Church of the liberties of the land.

216. **Thesis V.** *The education of children belongs by right to their parents.*

Explanation. This right belongs to parents primarily and *per se; per se—i. e.*, by the very fact that they are parents, though *per accidens* it may pass to others, as, *e. g.*, when the parents are dead, or if they are wholly unfit to exercise this right; *primarily—i. e.*, they possess this right before all others, and are responsible for the education of their children, even when they delegate part of their right to others who thus acquire a secondary right.

Proof 1. They who have a natural and indispensable duty to educate the young have the natural right to fulfill that duty. But parents have such a duty; therefore, they have the natural right to educate their children. That parents have such a duty is evident from the primary object of matrimony, which is not merely the generation of children, but especially the education of new members of the human family in a manner worthy of their rational nature.

Proof 2. The child has on his part an inalienable right to the means necessary for attaining his last end. Since education of some kind is such a means, he has a right to education. Now, surely this is not a vague, abstract right, but it is something determinate, and connotes determinate persons who are under positive obligation to care for that right. Such persons nature clearly points out; the parents are naturally the most closely related to the child; in them nature has implanted the enduring, patient love required for such a work; the child is naturally disposed to revere and love his parents and to receive their instructions and corrections with ready docility.

Proof 3. If education belonged by right to the State rather than to the parent, the former would have to perform all the functions of education, the feeding, clothing, and housing of the children no less than the office of instructing them in letters, morality, and religion. But such functions do not come within the range of the State's duties; attempts to assume them would be justly denounced as usurpations of personal rights. In particular: (*a*) Who does not feel that the State in its agents has no right to invade the home circle and there assume control, setting aside the wishes of parents and children? (*b*) The State is utterly incompetent, especially in a population of mixed creeds, to teach dogmatic religion; and yet without dogmatic religious teaching, morality is apt to be little more than a name.

217. Objections.

1. The State must control whatever bears on the public good; but such is the education of children. *Answer.* This principle, if followed out, would make us a nation of slaves; for it would destroy every personal right. Almost every act bears immediately or remotely on the public good; thus the State could regulate all details of food, clothing, and lodging, the choice of trade or profession, the selection of husband or wife; these matters, inasmuch as they affect the well-being of the citizens, are related to the common good. Accordingly, we reply to the objection: The State must control whatever bears on the public good —provided it does not go beyond its own province and usurp inalienable private rights, for the protection of which the State has been instituted.

2. The State is bound to secure what is so necessary for the public good as education. *Answer.* The State has no right to meddle in private matters that are well enough provided for. Its duty in such cases is to come forward and lend further assistance when private efforts are inadequate to avoid a great public evil or to procure a great public good. Now, education—especially that which is called elementary education—can be well enough imparted by parents and those whom they choose as aids in this work. The State may laudably encourage and assist private efforts: to be a patron of education is an honor; to usurp its functions is injustice.

3. But the State needs intelligent voters. *Answer.* The man in our times who cannot read and write is surely at a disadvantage; nevertheless, it is possible

for one to be very intelligent without book-learning. The State needs honest, conscientious voters; to obtain these, it must encourage sound religious instruction, but it need not control any form of education.

4. But the State should defend the rights of children; hence, it has a right to pass compulsory school laws. *Answer.* 1. The duty of defending children's rights could, at best, only entitle the State to compel parents to educate their children. 2. The education to which children have a *strict* right, is that which will fit them to attain their happiness in this world and the next. Now, this does not require a certain fixed amount of book-learning. Therefore, if parents choose to teach their child a trade, the latter has no further right to education that the State may defend.

218. The duties of children toward their parents are those of love, gratitude, honor, and obedience. Flowing directly from the mutual relations of parents and children, the first three of these duties remain always in full vigor. In regard to the duty of obedience, three periods of life are to be distinguished:

1. **During the years of imperfect judgment**, while the child constantly needs support and wise direction, he must allow himself to be trained by his parents with perfect docility. Hence, at this period, he owes them obedience in all things that are not opposed to the law of God. He must submit to his parents' correction and chastisement, in the infliction of which love ought to rule, accompanied by prudence, moderation, and firmness.

2. **When the judgment is matured,** yet the son or

daughter remains under the parental roof, the parents are to be obeyed in all things pertaining to the management of the home and the general good of the family. They must continue to watch over the morals of their children, to warn and reprove them whenever necessary, and even to enforce compliance with the laws of good behavior. They ought to assist their children to make a wise and prudent choice of a state of life, though they have no right to prescribe or dictate the state of life to be chosen, or the partner to be selected in marriage; nor can parents object to the adoption of a holier career in the religious or ecclesiastical state, unless they be in pressing need of their children's support. Man's first and highest allegiance is due not to his parents, but to God, and he has a perfect right to obey the Divine call to a holier manner of life. "He that loveth father or mother more than Me, is not worthy of Me." (Matt. x., 37.) Hence, it is apparent, also, that parents cannot rightfully prevent their children from embracing the true Faith.

3. When the grown-up son or daughter **withdraws from the parental home**, the duty of obedience ceases, but not the duties of love and reverence for parents, and of respect for their wisdom and advice. Moreover, all must assist their parents in case of need, and ever be to them a source of honor and consolation.

219. A complete family usually includes **servants**, who differ from other wage-earners by being permanently employed in domestic occupations. As such, they become inmates of the house, and, in a certain sense, members of the family. From this fact special rights and duties arise in

their regard with respect to the other members of the household; *e.g.*, they may be entrusted with delegated authority over the children of their employers. It is their duty to have the good of the family sincerely at heart: and, on the other hand, they are entitled not only to their salary, but also to special love and care, particularly in times of illness. Every one is bound by the natural law to see to the moral and physical welfare of those belonging to his own household.

220. We know from history that at the dawn of Christianity nearly half the human race was in a state of **slavery**. In the mildest meaning of the term, a slave is a human being bound for life to work for his master without other remuneration than his support, possessing no rights except those that are inalienable. *Inalienable rights* are such as are intimately connected with the attainment of our last end. They are the rights to life, limbs, health, surroundings favorable to morality, and in general all those aids to eternal happiness of which a man cannot justly deprive himself, since by so doing he would infringe God's rights to his service. Slavery thus limited may, perhaps, in certain special circumstances, contain no violation of strict right, and, therefore, no injustice; yet, it ever has been an evil, usually far greater than squalid poverty; and it has occasioned countless abuses of the most deplorable kind. Hence, the Church has always labored—and with unfailing success—to mitigate and finally to suppress it. To the general satisfaction, slavery has disappeared from all Christian lands. There is no reason, therefore, for treating the subject further.

CHAPTER III.

CIVIL SOCIETY.

221. **Civil society** may be defined as a union of many such persons as are their own masters, *sui juris*, joined together for the purpose of protecting their rights and securing their temporal happiness. In the present chapter we shall consider the nature and the origin of civil society, and the exercise of civil functions.

ARTICLE 1. THE NATURE AND THE ORIGIN OF CIVIL SOCIETY.

222. The nature of civil society can be best understood from a detailed examination into its **constituent notes**, namely: 1. Its end or purpose, 2. The units composing it, 3. The authority governing it, 4. The means employed to obtain its end.

§ 1. *The End of Civil Society.*

223. 1. We have seen in a preceding chapter (No. 199) that society, or association of some kind, is natural to man, and, consequently, that it is an institution of God. The society first in the order of nature is the family, or domestic society, and next in order comes civil society, or the State.

The necessity of civil society is obvious: when many families live in proximity, they are forced to have intercourse of some sort with one another. In the course of time it will come to pass, as each family has chiefly its own interests at heart, that many of these families will not be moderate in their aspirations, their claims, and their efforts at aggrandizement. Hence, unless they be united for the purpose of securing public peace and the protection of personal rights, they will be frequently at variance, and even in deadly strife with one another.

224. The preservation of peace among its members is the **primary end** of civil society. United by a common bond, men can render great assistance to one another in securing, with comparative ease, the comfort and happiness of all; and opportunities for the development and exercise of the human faculties are thus afforded which would be impossible without such an association. The complex end of civil society is clearly stated in the preamble to the Constitution of the United States, which reads thus: "We, the people of the United States, in order to form a more perfect union, establish justice, ensure domestic tranquillity, provide for the common defense, promote the general welfare, and secure the blessings of liberty to ourselves and our posterity, do ordain and establish this Constitution for the United States of America."

225. Civil society, we repeat, is **natural to man**, and, consequently, owes its institution to the Creator. It is natural, because it is the outcome of man's natural tendencies and is necessary for the development and application of his highest powers. Without civil society, men could not lead lives worthy of their rational nature and their ultimate destiny. The theory of Hobbes and of Rousseau, that man is naturally a savage, perpetually at war with his fellow-men, and that society is an afterthought, something artificial superadded to his nature, is as opposed to historical facts as it is degrading to the human race.

§ 2. *The units of which civil society is composed.*

226. When certain families have entered into association for mutual aid and protection, the domestic relations in each family are manifestly not altered thereby: the family continues to be a natural society; each family is a moral person, the father acting for all the members. Hence **the units composing civil society** are not individual men, women, and children, but the families, or the heads of families. The wives and children are indeed members of the State, though not directly; they are members of the families that make up the State, and they are represented in the State by the heads of the families to which they severally belong. It is neither necessary nor desirable for the common good that the State should deal directly with them, ignoring the natural organization of the domestic society. Unmarried men, who are properly qualified by age and civil condition, *i. e.*, who have attained their majority and are their own masters, *sui juris*, share with heads of families in the enjoyment of civil rights.

§ 3. *Civil Authority.*

227. That the common good may be attained, the members of which civil society is made up often stand in need of direction, and sometimes of compulsion. The power thus to direct and compel is called **civil authority**; it is, as it were, the soul or animating principle of the body politic. What rights should belong to this authority must be inferred from its purpose, which is the attainment of the end of civil society. Civil authority, therefore, is to possess all those rights which are necessary to direct, and even compel, the citizens to tend towards the end of the State, *i. e.*, public peace, the protection of rights, the more perfect attainment

of happiness for all, provided the means employed be consistent with individual rights.

228. But may not the common good require **the sacrifice of individual or private rights?** As the common good consists principally in the defense of the private rights of individuals and families, it cannot require such a sacrifice. Exceptions in this matter are more apparent than real. Yet, aside from the forfeiture of personal rights or privileges for certain misdeeds, cases may arise in which individuals or families have to forego private advantages in order to serve the common good: as when a citizen is called upon to expose his life for the defense of his country. In this case his right is not violated; the State does not take away his life, but it obliges him to expose himself to danger for a greater good, in accordance with the demands of duty.

229. **In levying taxes,** the State distributes the common burden of expenses incurred for the public good. The right of eminent domain (No. 177) suspends a private right according to the principles explained in a preceding book (No. 121). The tendency of certain agitators in politics and political economy is to extend the powers of the State beyond all just limits, to the prejudice of private rights. This tendency, whether it is manifested in the advocacy of unjust taxation, in special class legislation, or in meddling with parental rights of education, is directly at variance with the purposes of civil government, and opposed to the spirit of our Constitution. Civil government exists for the welfare of the people and the protection of private rights. When, therefore, the government usurps the rights of individuals, it becomes a form of tyranny, quiet submission to which is not patriotism, but slavery.

230. **Whence comes the authority of the State?** The

question may refer to civil authority in the abstract or in the concrete. Civil authority *in the concrete* regards the particular form of government which a particular State or nation has come to assume. It is evidently a matter of historical fact: certain events have brought about the assumption of that manner of government.

Supposing now that a State or government exists, we may inquire whence it derives authority; *i. e.*, the right to govern its subjects. This latter is a consideration of authority *in the abstract*, and is an ethical question.

231. **Thesis VI.** *Civil authority is derived from God, and can impose conscientious obligations.*

Proof. As in every society (No. 196), so in civil society, authority is necessary; it is the very form or animating principle of civil society (No. 227). Now, God is the founder of civil society, since it is natural to man; and God necessarily wills that everything He makes shall possess all powers necessary for the purposes for which He made it. But authority is necessary for the purpose of civil society; therefore, it possesses this authority from God.

From this principle, it follows that civil government can impose obligations in conscience. Authority means the moral right to govern. Now, such a right implies on the part of the governed the moral obligation to obey. Nevertheless, the authority thus bestowed is limited to those purposes for which it was intrusted to the State—namely, to procure the end of civil government by just means. Hence, an unlawful use of authority imposes no moral obligation.

232. It has been much debated whether civil authority comes **immediately from God to the ruler, or through the medium of the people**, by whom it is intrusted to the rulers. Certainly, it can hardly be said that such authority resides

with an unorganized multitude; yet, as soon as the community has become an organized body, it has the moral power of civil government. It may intrust this power to one or more persons, and it may place restrictions upon these both with regard to the time and the manner of exercising the authority thus bestowed.

233. One thing is certain—namely, that civil authority is **not a mere collection of private rights** intrusted by all the individuals of a community to the management of one or more chosen members. The civil power has the right to inflict the death penalty (No. 249) in punishment of enormous crimes. But such a right could not belong to a merely voluntary association of individuals, since they cannot give to any person or persons a right which they do not possess. Therefore, civil authority is not a mere collection of private rights. This principle is further explained in the following thesis:

234. **Thesis VII.** *The doctrine of the social contract maintained by Rousseau is illogical.*

Explanation. According to the fanciful theory of the "social contract" devised by Jean Jacques Rousseau, the citizens, when they obey the authority of the State, obey themselves or fulfill their own commands; for civil authority he declared to be nothing else than the free union of individual wills. He supposed that the members of a community have agreed to intrust the exercise of their individual rights to one or more men, who thus become their agents for the administration of these associated rights, just like the agents of a business firm, and who may be, like such agents, dismissed at the pleasure of their employers. As forms of government have existed from time immemorial, the supposed contract must have been entered into by our remote ancestors,

Proof 1. Either the citizens are bound by the agreement of their ancestors to a civil compact or they are not so bound. If such an obligation exists, they do not render obedience to themselves, as Rousseau would have it, but to their ancestors; hence, they would be bound by a will not their own. If, however, no such obligation exists, then there is no civil authority at all; for that is no authority which every one is free at any moment to set aside. There can be no true right to command where there is no corresponding duty to obey.

Proof 2. This theory could never explain the right, admitted by all nations, of inflicting capital punishment; for no one can give to another what he does not himself possess— the right to take away his life.

§ 4. *The Means Employed by Civil Authority.*

235. The means employed to obtain the end of civil government are of **three kinds**:
   1. Acts commanded as necessary for this end, such as the payment of taxes, or the raising and equipment of armies in time of war.
   2. Acts forbidden as injurious to private rights or to the common good. On both these points there is need of great care that, by the promotion of certain lawful objects or the protection of certain rights, other rights be not violated, especially those of a more sacred character; this would defeat the very purpose for which civil government exists.
   3. The organization of the government, or the civil polity which is to direct the means to the end.

236. There are **various forms of organization**:
   1. The *monarchical*, in which all civil power is vested

in one man, whether he be called king or emperor or by any other title.

2. The *aristocratic*, in which power is vested in a few individuals or families.

3. The *democratic*, in which the people hold the power; it is then usually administered by representatives whom the people have chosen. These are the simple forms of government organization. *Mixed* forms are those in which the simple forms are variously combined. In the British Government, for instance, the supreme power is vested in the crown—king or queen —and in Parliament, which consists of the House of Lords, as the aristocratic element, and the House of Commons, as the democratic element, the members of the latter House being elected by the people.

237. Practically, that form of government is **the best for any people** which is best adapted to obtain for them the end or purpose of civil power; that form, namely, which, account being taken of the character, traditions, and various circumstances of the people, is best suited for the defense of their private rights, for the maintenance of peace at home and abroad, and for the development of the country's resources; which will thus contribute to the common happiness on earth, and enable every member of the community to attain his last end.

ARTICLE II. THE FUNCTIONS OF CIVIL GOVERNMENT.

238. To fulfill its purposes, civil government must exercise **three functions,** namely: the *legislative*, in the making of laws; the *judiciary*, in the application of the laws to particular cases; the *executive*, in carrying laws and judgments into effect.

All three functions may be exercised by one person or body of men; but in this country they are intrusted to three distinct departments: the legislative to Congress, the judiciary to the law courts, the executive to the President.

§ 1. *Legislation.*

239. Since the State derives its authority from the moral law, it can, as we have shown, bind its subjects in conscience to observe its enactments (No. 231). In order to possess this binding force, **such enactments must be just** (*ibid.*); therefore, they must fulfill all the conditions required for just laws (No. 81). Hence, one readily perceives how false, when applied to legislative acts, the common saying may be, "The voice of the people is the voice of God." An unjust law enacted, even with perfect unanimity, by an entire nation would have in itself no binding force; *a fortiori*, it has no such power if passed by a mere majority. In fact, a majority may be just as tyrannical as a despotic monarch. Since laws are, by their nature, directions for future acts, they cannot justly brand an action as guilty which before the passage of such laws was considered innocent; nor can they justly increase the punishment for an act already committed. Hence, the Constitution of the United States forbids the enactment by Congress of *ex post facto* laws.

240. Though the civil authority has power to bind the conscience, yet not every purely civil law imposes such obligation. For laws have no greater binding effect than their authors intend to impose; nor can the obligation exceed the requirements of the common good. Some laws accomplish all the purposes for which they were enacted, if the transgressor is obliged to pay the appointed penalty when caught

in the forbidden act; and the legislator is often content with this kind of sanction without being willing to lay a moral obligation on the conscience. Such laws are styled **merely penal laws.** In practice, it is often not easy to determine which laws are merely penal. Evidently, however, those laws oblige in conscience the violation of which would be positively injurious to the common good.

241. The office of legislation is to direct the acts of the citizens to the attainment of the end proper to civil society. That end includes public order, defense of private rights, and development of material and mental resources for the common good. Hence, **legislation must take care—**

1. *To ward off physical evils* from the country, *e. g.*, contagious diseases. Therefore it has power to use the means necessary for such purpose, *e. g.*, the enactment of sanitary regulations, the establishment of quarantine, etc.
2. *To ward off moral evils*, such as the dissemination of false doctrines that weaken morality, undermine society, and attack natural religion. Hence, too, the State has a clear right to put just restrictions on license of speech and of the press. The public profanation of Sunday, indecent theatricals, houses of debauch tend to degrade the standard of public and private morality, and, consequently, are subject to legislative action. On the other hand, religion, the chief safeguard of morals, ought to be at all times countenanced and actively protected.
3. *To protect individual rights*, such as the rights of minors, of orphans, of those concerned in contracts, in last wills, etc.
4. *To forward material improvements*, such as high-

ways, bridges, watercourses, harbors, and all such works generally as are useful to the country at large and too vast for private enterprise.

5. *To promote mental development*, by encouraging education and assisting educational institutions, especially those devoted to the teaching of the highest branches; for education contributes largely to the common good, and higher studies in particular, though pursued by the few, redound to the welfare of the people generally.

242. In many undertakings the State ought **to aid but not to supplant private enterprise**, assuming the lead when individuals and corporations can advance no further, subsidizing important works that affect the general welfare, without exercising a monopoly or competing with private efforts. The tendency of Socialism is to substitute State control for private enterprise in many departments of business, without any benefit to the common good. Thus, instead of being a protector, the State would become a usurper of private rights, and in this way defeat the purpose of its existence.

§ 2. *The Judiciary.*

243. **The task of the judiciary is twofold:**
1. To settle disputes between rival claimants: this is done in the civil courts.
2. To prosecute, in criminal courts, persons charged with violating the law, and, in case of their conviction, to award the penalty appointed for the transgression. The settlement of civil disputes is often submitted by the disputing parties to arbiters chosen by themselves. An *arbiter* differs from a judge in this, that the latter

acts in virtue of the sovereign power of the State, and, therefore, possesses authority over the parties concerned, while an arbiter has no rights in the matter under dispute except such as are conceded to him by the litigants. From the decision of the lower courts appeal may be made in important cases to higher courts. But there must be, in the nature of things, a *supreme court*, from whose decision there can be no appeal. Though even this higher tribunal may err, nevertheless the public good requires that its decisions shall be final.

244. The courts are **guided by existing laws**, the expediency of which is no matter for their consideration; their work is the interpretation and application of existing laws to special cases. Yet certain courts are sometimes called upon to decide whether a given enactment is truly a law, whether it has all the requirements of a just law (No. 81). If an enactment is evidently unjust or is openly at variance with the Constitution of the country, it is not a law, and judges cannot justly enforce it.

245. The preservation of public order, one of the primary functions of civil society, necessitates **the punishment of social crimes.** Now, a social crime is an outward disturbance of civil society by the violation of a strict right of our fellow-men. Evil acts in which injury is done to those persons only who freely take part in them, do not violate a strict right of any man, and are, therefore, not subject to the punishments of civil authority.

It is for the legislative power to appoint the punishment of crimes, for the judiciary to award the punishment in individual cases, for the executive to inflict it, or, in exceptional circumstances, at the discretion of the official holding the necessary authority, to remit or commute the penalty.

246. **Thesis VIII.** *Civil society has the right to punish social crimes.*

Proof. Every natural society has a right to those means which, in the ordinary course of events, are necessary for it to obtain its ends; but the punishment of social crimes is such a means for civil society. Therefore civil society has the right to punish social crimes.

247. Let us consider **how and why such punishment is necessary** in order that civil society may attain its end.

> 1. That end is the maintenance of social order. To secure this, it is necessary that advantage and pleasure be consequent on the observance of order. But the criminal disturbs the order of things by seeking to make advantage and pleasure consequent upon disorder. Accordingly, justice requires, for the restoration of right order which he has disturbed, that he shall lose advantages or feel pain. For this purpose, then, various kinds and degrees of punishment are needed to match the various kinds of evil doings and the various grades of guilt. Hence, one purpose of legal punishment is **expiation**.
>
> 2. The end of civil society is likewise to guard rights from violation; but this cannot be done unless offenders be punished in a manner **to deter others** from following their evil example; the penalty should, for this purpose, be proportioned to the crime.
>
> 3. The criminal himself needs **correction**, *i. e.*, by the bitter medicine of pain he is to be induced to give up his vicious practices, and kept from disturbing the social order in the future.

248. Thus a threefold reason exists for the infliction of legal punishment; it is *expiatory, deterrent*, and *medicinal*. In domestic society, punishment is primarily medicinal for the correction of the offender, yet at times it may be deterrent for others. In civil society, punishment is chiefly expiatory and deterrent, and it need not be medicinal.

249. **Thesis IX.** *Civil society has the right to inflict the death penalty for enormous crimes.*

Explanation. We know from Revelation that God has bestowed this right upon civil authority; we maintain here that it belongs to civil society by the principles of natural reason.

Proof. The means employed by civil society must be sufficient to attain its end. Now, in many cases, nothing less than capital punishment is sufficient to attain that end. For, (*a*) There are criminals so depraved and so indifferent to other forms of punishment that the death penalty alone can deter them from committing enormous crimes. (*b*) Some crimes, such as deliberate murder, treason, or parricide, disturb social order to such an extent that capital punishment alone approaches a proportionate atonement.

250. **Objections:**
1. Man is too noble a being to be slaughtered as a warning to others. *Answer.* Such certainly he is if he has done no wrong; not, however, if he has degraded himself by a monstrous crime.
2. The present doctrine would justify "Lynch law," and mob violence, which are evident evils. *Answer.* A mob has no authority to inflict death: civil society receives such authority from God, its founder.
3. Every man has an inalienable right to his life; therefore the State cannot condemn him to death. *Answer.*

When we say that a right is inalienable, we mean that no one can take it away except God and one delegated by Him for that purpose; now the State has a commission from God to inflict the death penalty for enormous crimes.

4. In some States the death penalty has been abolished; therefore it is not necessary. *Answer.* That consequent does not follow from the antecedent. It is not clear that the purposes of civil government are sufficiently attained in those States. If they are, it is owing to special circumstances, and constitutes an exception to a general rule.

5. Desperate men are not restrained by fear of the death penalty. *Answer.* Nevertheless it is the most potent restraint that the State can use; besides, such men are prevented by the prompt infliction of the penalty from multiplying their enormities. Moreover, few criminals have been found so hardened as not eagerly to desire a commutation of capital punishment to imprisonment for life.

§ 3. *The Executive.*

251. In addition to the legislative and judicial departments, a country requires for its government *executive officers*, *an armed force*, and a *treasury* for the remuneration of public services. Those officials whose duty it is to carry the laws into effect form **the executive department**, which is in some respects dependent upon the two other departments. The President of the United States is the chief executive officer of the nation; at the same time he is at the head of the legislative department, holding the power of *veto* and giving validity

to the enactments of Congress by affixing his signature thereto. The President is also the official embodiment of the majesty and authority of the nation.

252. **The public officers** ought to be chosen or appointed from those who, by their knowledge, ability, fidelity, and integrity, are well qualified to procure the common good. The practice of distributing offices as the spoils of party victory among the unworthy and incompetent, is a gross violation of distributive justice and a serious injury to the State.

253. The **treasury** is supplied either by *direct taxation*, *i.e.*, by taxes imposed on the property of the individual citizens, or by *indirect taxation, i. e.*, revenues and duties paid for manufactured and imported goods. The right of taxation is based upon the need of the government to defray public expenses incurred for the common good; hence, the taxes levied should not exceed these expenses. The assessment of taxes for each class of the citizens ought, as far as is practicable, to be proportioned to the benefits received therefrom. Thus, each citizen receives from the State an equivalent for the taxes he pays, and no one is forced to labor for another without just compensation. This rule does not prevent the taxation of the rich to supply assistance to the needy poor. The honest poor have a right, as human beings, to live in decent comfort, and, if they cannot succeed in doing so by their own exertions, they must be aided by the wealthy members of the community. It is even necessary for the common good that no class of the people should be driven by want to discontent and desperation.

254. **The armed force** required by civil society consists usually of:

1. The *police*, a body of men who exercise a constant

guardianship over public tranquillity and the rights of individuals.

2. The *militia*, or civic troops, intended chiefly for the protection of the State against the insubordination of its own subjects.

3. The *regular army*, whose main purpose is defense against foreign foes.

As personal danger naturally accompanies the work of armed men, these are bound, when the occasion requies it, to expose themselves even to death in the performance of their duty. In the use of armed force, nations approach nearest to ideal perfection when this use is brought within the narrowest limits, while at the same time the public peace is vigorously maintained. Accordingly, the people of the United States have reason to congratulate themselves that public order reigns so extensively, though the army is comparatively diminutive, the militia seldom needed, and the police rarely compelled to make use of deadly weapons.

CHAPTER IV.

INTERNATIONAL LAW.

255. All the members of mankind naturally constitute **one universal society** (No. 198), of which God Himself is the founder, ruler, lawgiver, and judge. In this universal society a great variety of rights and duties has place. Thus far we have considered those of individuals (Book II.), those of domestic society (Book III., C. II.), and those which arise in civil society (C. III.). Lastly, we are to examine the rights and duties which issue from the relations of independent civil societies to one another. These rights and duties are regulated by *international law*.

256. **International law** is defined by James Madison, fourth President of the United States, as "Consisting of those rules which reason deduces as consonant to justice, from the nature of the society existing among independent nations; with such definitions and modifications as may be established by general consent" (Wheaton's Elements of International Law, C. I.). As a distinct code, it is of modern origin; for within recent times intercourse, chiefly commercial, between the nations of the earth has attained such proportions and is become so intricate that regulations governing it have assumed vast importance.

Formerly international law constituted in Philosophy a branch of what was called *jus gentium*, the law of nations, defined by Suarez as "That which is laid down by reason among all mankind and is observed by nearly all nations:" it treated of both civil and international right.

257. As now understood, international law comprises **two parts**, indicated in Madison's definition, namely:
1. What reason requires, *i. e.*, *the natural rights*, and
2. Such definitions and modifications of this as may be established by general consent, *i. e.*, acquired or *conventional rights*. The latter may be determined *explicitly*, by contracts among the nations, or *implicitly*, by custom so well established as to be considered binding on all civilized countries.

258. By a **nation** we here mean an independent civil government; the several States of the Union, though sovereign States—possessed of the right of the sword and other attributes of sovereignty—are, nevertheless, not so many nations, because not independent in many respects; but all together constitute one nation, represented by our central national government. Evidently a nation here does not mean a race, as it does when we speak of the Celtic nation. Nor does it mean a geographical division; for this may contain various nations, *e. g.*, Spain and Portugal. Again, one nation may be made up of diverse races, as is the case in Austria or Great Britain; and one race may be divided among various nations or governments, as is exemplified in the Teutonic race.

259. **The principles underlying all international law are the following:**
1. That every man must love all other men (Nos. 149, 198).
2. That every independent civil society is a *moral person*, and, as such, possessed of definite rights, which must be respected by all other persons, physical and moral. For a person is properly a complete substance endowed with intellect (Mental Philosophy, No. 55),

a being, therefore, capable of having rights and duties. Civil society, inasmuch as it is complete and independent in its own line, and is a collection of intellectual units, is called a moral person; as such it is the embodiment of all the private rights pertaining to its members. Besides, since civil society is natural to man, it has a natural right to exist and to use whatever just means are necessary for attaining its end.

260. Since the rights of a nation flow from its essence as a complete civil society, **all nations stand on an equal footing** with regard to natural rights. Hence, the greater powers have no more natural right to lord it over less potent nations than strong men have a right to neglect and abuse the rights of infants. In particular:

1. No nation may enter the territory of another nation without the consent of the latter.
2. One nation has no right to interfere with the internal workings of another government. Hence, foreign powers have no right to encourage or assist subjects rebelling against legitimate authority.
3. Yet one nation has a right to assist another nation if the latter asks such assistance. The principle of *non-intervention*, in the sense that one nation is not allowed to render the aid requested by another nation in distress, is unjust. In effect, this principle allows a robber nation to despoil its victim, and helps rebel subjects to oppose lawfully established authority.

261. **The natural rights of a nation**, which all are obliged to respect, are chiefly as follows:

1. The right of preserving its existence as a nation. Such existence implies four conditions: union among

the citizens, legitimate authority, independence, the dignity of a moral person invested with sovereignty.

2. The right to maintain civil order among its members. This implies: the dependence of the subjects on their rulers, a just administration of the commonwealth, concord among the citizens.

3. The right to acquire new territory, whether by treaty or by first occupancy, etc., provided no prior rights be violated.

4. The right of dominion over its water-courses, which include such an extent of the adjacent seas as is necessary for the security and prosperity of its citizens. Conflicting claims must be settled by treaties, customs, etc.

5. The right to honorable recognition by other nations and by men generally. This implies the sacredness of embassies, etc., a right which has always been acknowledged by all civilized nations.

6. The right to develop its resources, material and intellectual, and generally the right to promote all that tends to public and private prosperity without prejudice to private rights.

7. Lastly, the right to manage its own affairs; hence, to determine changes in its manner of administration, and to settle difficulties with its own subjects without interference or contradiction on the part of other States.

262. Nature has established no human authority superior to that of national governments; hence, there is no higher human power to enforce the observance of the moral law by nations and to decide conflicting international claims. A **universal arbiter** to decide contests between nations were

indeed desirable. Such the Supreme Pontiff was among Christian nations in the ages of Faith. In special cases, he has lately been called upon to act in a similar capacity, to the great advantage of justice, peace, and civilization.

263. When arbitration cannot be agreed upon by contesting nations, recourse is had to **war**, to which, as a last resort, they have an undoubted right. That a war may be justifiable, **these conditions** are required:

1. That a nation's claims are just, important, moderate, and certain.
2. That every reasonable effort has been made in vain to settle the dispute by peaceable means.
3. That war offers a fair prospect of success; for no one is justified in choosing the greater of two evils; least of all can those in authority do so, for they are the guardians of their subjects' rights.
4. That war be undertaken, as Cicero says, only as a means to bring about a just peace.

264. **The manner of waging war** should be conformable to the approved usages of civilized nations. To be effective, it necessitates destruction of life and property, confiscations, sieges, blockades, battles, bombardments, and all the horrors unavoidably connected with such measures. **But it does not justify:**

1. Any useless or wanton violence or destruction by which the final settlement is not furthered; for instance, the direct killing or ill-treating of non-combatants, such as women and children.
2. The killing of prisoners or wounded soldiers who have no more power to injure.
3. The use of means universally execrated as unneces-

sarily cruel, such as envenomed weapons, poisoned wells, etc.

4. The use of means that are in themselves unjust, such as lying, perjury, and solicitations to treason.

5. The continuation of hostilities when a settlement has been made possible.

265. **The victorious nation has the right:**

1. To possess the object for which the war was waged, and to which it had all along a just claim.

2. To exact compensation for the damages sustained in the war.

3. To provide for its future security against a dangerous foe. This may even necessitate the permanent subjection of the defeated nation. Moderation, justice, and humanity must ever prevail.

266. It is **the tendency of Christian civilization** to cultivate universal good-will and forbearance, not only among Christian nations, but towards all mankind. It has gradually removed the most revolting usages of warfare—the useless slaughter of the vanquished, the enslaving of the conquered, with their wives and children, the wanton destruction of property, the lawless plundering and sacking of cities, the inhuman treatment of the weak, the aged and the young. Thus it has limited, as far as is possible, the horrors of war to those actually in arms. This same tendency has introduced tender care of the wounded, respectful burial of the dead, a chivalrous treatment of all parties in the midst of hostilities, and has lessened ill-feeling after the re-establishment of peace. Its greatest triumph has been the prevention of active hostilities; so that war is now an exceptional occurrence, whereas it used to be the common occupation of nations. We may hope that the still wider prevalence of

Christian principles and of correct views on the purposes and duties of civil society will gradually enable the nations to dispense with war altogether, by deferring all international contests to the arbitration of the most worthy personage on earth, the Vicar of the Prince of Peace.

THE END.

ALPHABETICAL INDEX.

The numbers refer to the paragraphs.

Abraham, 89, 154.
Abrogation of laws, 87.
Accession, 182.
Accountability, 54 to 60; hinderances to, 61 to 67.
Acquired rights, 119.
Acquisition of property, 170 to 182.
Action, external, 52.
Adoration, 124 to 126.
Agnostics, 38, 138.
Alienable rights, 119.
Anger, 69.
Arbiter, 243, 262, 266.
Aristocracy, 236.
Armed force, 254.
Authority, 139, 196; parental, 211; civil, 227 to 229; its origin, 230 to 234; means, 235.
Aversion, 69.

Beatific vision, 33.
Beatitude, 26 to 35.
Benevolence, love of, 140.
Binding the will, 54, 56, 117, 240.
Blasphemy, 127.
Brave, 79.

Capital punishment, 233, 249, 250.
Cardinal virtues, 74.
Caution, 76.
Celibacy, 201.

Circumstances, 49.
Civil Society, 221; notes of, 222; end, 223, 224; necessity, 225; units, 226; authority, 227 to 234.
Civilized warfare, 266.
Clear-sightedness, 76.
Communism, 179.
Concupiscence, 65, 78.
Conflict of rights, 120, 121, 228.
Congress, 238.
Connatural rights, 119.
Conscience, 80, 95 to 106, 240.
Constitution of U. S., 175, 224, 239.
Contract, 183; gratuitous, 184; onerous, 187; conditions of, 188; social, 234; protection of, 241.
Courage, 69, 79, 144.
Courts of law, 239, 243, 244.
Cowardice, 79.
Craftiness, 76.
Crime, 245.

Damage repaired, 181.
Danger, 145.
David, 162.
Death penalty, 233, 249, 250.
Democracy, 236.
Derogation, 87.
Desire, 69, 141.
Despondency, 69.
Determinants of morality, 46 to 52.

163

Dispensation, 87.
Divine law, 82.
Divorce, 206 to 208.
Domestic society, 200 to 220.
Doubtful conscience, 99 to 106.
Duel, 167 to 169.
Duties, see "Rights"; to ourselves, 142, 143; to fellow-men, 146 to 149; to enemies, 150; of children, 218.

Education, 213 to 220, 241.
Eminent domain, 177, 229.
Emotions, 68.
Employer, 189 to 192.
End, 6 to 8; kinds of, 9 to 12; last, 13; mediate, 17, 20; attainable, 27, 28; subjective, objective, material, formal, 24; of act, 48; and means, 48, 164.
Equivocation, 154.
Eternal, law, 83; punishment, 109 to 112.
Evil, 37 to 39, 45.
Example, 158.
Excuse from moral law, 85.
Executive, 238, 251 to 254.
Expiation, 248.
Exposing life, 145.
Ex post facto law, 239.
External action, 52.

Faculties, higher and lower, 18, 35; tend to God, 21; need society, 199.
Faith, 124, 129.
False theories of morality, 44.
Fear, 66, 69.
Filial piety, 75.
Finding lost articles, 182.
Formula of natural law, 84.
Fortitude, 74, 79.
Friendship, 140.

Glory of God, 22.

God, tendency to, 14; how? 15 to 17; man's last end, 20 to 24, 32, 41; binds us, 54, 55; duties to, 122 to 142.
Golden mean, 77.
Good, true, 8, 18; kinds of, 19, 40; and bad, 37 to 39, 42; radical notion of, 40.
Goods of earth, 35.
Government, civil, 235 to 237; functions, 238 to 254.
Grant of land, 177.
Gratitude, 75.

Habit, 72.
Happiness, 25 to 35.
Hate, 60.
Heroism, 148.
Hinderances to accountability, 61 to 67.
Hobbes, 44, 225.
Homicide, 159.
Honor, 143, 165, 166, 169.
Hope, 69, 141.
Human, acts, 2, 5, 7, 36, 45; law, 82; binding, 93, 94.
Husband, 211.
Huxley's theory of morals, 38.

Idolatry, 127.
Ignorance, 62 to 64.
Immortality, 112.
Immutability of natural law, 87 to 89.
Impiety, 127.
Imputable, 53.
Inalienable rights, 119, 216, 220, 250.
Indifference in religion, 134 to 136.
Indifferent act, 45.
Indirect will, 50, 51.
Infallibility, 139.
Infanticide, 164.
Instinct, 44.

Alphabetical Index.   165

Intellect, 143.
Interest, 87.
International law, 176, 255; defined, 256; parts, 257; principles, 259, 260.
Intolerance, 130.
Israelites, 89.

Joy, 69.
Judiciary, 238, 243 to 250.
Jus gentium, 176, 256.
Justice, 75.

Knowledge of natural law, 90 to 92.

Laborer, 189 to 192.
Landed property, 173.
Last, end, 9, 13 to 16; will, 185, 186.
Law, defined, 80; requisites, 81; kinds, 82; natural, 83 to 92; human, 93. 94; of nations, 176; just, 239; penal, 240; international, 176, 255 to 260.
Laxists, 104.
Legislation, 238 to 242.
Leo XIII., quoted, 190, 192.
Liceity, 104, 105.
License of speech and press, 241.
Lie, 153, 156, 157.
Life, right to, 160.
Lost articles, 182.
Love, 69; of God, 124, 140, 141; due to others, 146 to 149; due to enemies, 150; degrees of, 151.

Madison, 256.
Magnanimity, 79.
Mandeville, 44.
Manslaughter, 159.
Marriage, 200; ends of, 201, 202; unity, 203 to 205; indissolubility, 206 to 208.
Materialists, 38, 138.

Mathathias, 162.
Mean, golden, 77.
Means, 48, 164.
Mental reservation, 155, 157.
Merit, 57 to 61.
Minors, 188.
Miracle, 131, 132.
Misery, 23.
Monarchy, 226.
Moral, good, 19, 39, 40; sense, 44.
Moral Philosophy, defined, 1; founded on Mental, 3; divided, 4.
Morality, 36; essence of, 37 to 43; false theories, 44; determinants, 46 to 52.
Mortification, 78.
Moses, 162.
Murder, 159 to 162.
Mystery, 129, 130.

Nation, 258.
Natural law, 82, 83; formula of, 84; no excuse from, 85; precepts of, 86; immutable, eternal, 87 to 89; known, 90 to 92.
Necessity, extreme, 149.

Object of act, 47.
Occupancy, first, 174 to 176, 182.
Offices, 197, 252.
Ought, 39.
Ownership, 170; titles to, 171 to 179; violations of, 180.

Paley, 44.
Pantheists, 38, 138.
Parental authority, 211.
Passions, 68 to 71, 143.
Patience, 79.
Penal law, 240.
Perfection, kinds of, 35.
Piety, filial, 75.
Plato, 144.
Pleasure, 19.

Alphabetical Index.

Polyandry, 204.
Polygamy, 205.
Positive laws, 82.
Positivists, 38, 138.
Prayer, 128.
Precepts, affirmative and negative, 86.
Preference, love of, 141.
Prescription, 182.
Press, license of, 241.
Prior rights, 118, 123.
Private enterprise, 242.
Probability, 96, 98, 104.
Promulgation, 81.
Property, 170 to 174; modes of acquiring, 171 to 179; transfer of, 183 to 186.
Prophecy, 131, 132.
Punishment, eternal, 109 to 112; civil, 247, 248; capital, 249, 250.
Pusillanimity, 76.

Rashness, 79.
Reasoning, 139.
Religion, 75, 124; one true, 136; in education, 214.
Repairing damage, 181.
Reservation, mental, 155, 157.
Responsibility, 63.
Restitution, 180.
Resurrection, 29, 30.
Revelation, 129 to 131; kinds of, 137, 138.
Right and wrong, 37 to 39.
Rights, of God, 55, 123; of life and death, 160; of societies, 195; of domestic society, 209; of civil society, 227 to 234; of nations, 259 to 269.
Rights and duties, 113 to 116; from God, 117; priority of, 118; kinds, 119, 122; in conflict, 120, 121, 228; of children, 216, 217.

Rigorists, 104.
Robbery, 180.
Rousseau, 225, 234.

Sacrifice, 128.
Sadness, 69.
Sanction, 107 to 112.
Scandal, 158.
Self-defense, 163, 164.
Self-distrust, 76.
Sense, moral, 44.
Separation *a toro*, 207.
Servants, 219.
Simplicity, 76.
Sin, mortal and venial, 43; punishment of, 112.
Slavery, 220.
Social contract, 234.
Socialism, 179, 242.
Society, 193; kinds, 194; authority, 195 to 197; universal, 198; natural to man, 198; domestic, 200 to 220; civil, 221 to 254; international, 255.
Speech, license of, 241.
Spencer's theory of morals, 38, 44.
State, control of education, 215, 217; rights regarding matrimony, 210.
Stoics, 71.
Strikes, 191.
Suicide, 144, 145.
Sui juris, 221, 226.
Summum bonum, 109; see "Beatitude."
Sunday, 241.

Taxation, 177, 229.
Temperance, 74, 78.
Theft, 88, 180.
Theories of morality, 44.
Timidity, 76.
Titles to ownership, 171 to 179.

Transfer of property, 183 to 186.
Treasury, 253.
Tutiorists, 104.

Unions, labor, 191.
United States, 175, 224, 239.
Useful, 19, 44.
Utilitarianism, 44.

Vices, 72; against religion, 127.
Victorious nation, 165.
Violation of ownership, 180.
Violence, 67.

Virtues, 72 to 79.
Virtus in medio, 77.
Vox populi, 44, 239.

Wages, 189 to 192.
War, 263 to 266.
Wife, 200, 205, 212.
Will, 7, 68, 74; indirect, 50, 51; last, 185, 186.
Worship, 125, 126.
Wrong, see "Right."

Zeno, 71.

www.ingramcontent.com/pod-product-compliance
Lightning Source LLC
Chambersburg PA
CBHW030242170426
43202CB00009B/593